What people are saying about …

Follow

"For decades, Floyd McClung has been at the forefront of a generation passionately following Christ, equipping them to know Him deeply and serve Him around the globe. *Follow* paves the way for practical and powerful engagement by anyone seeking to make Jesus famous among all nations!"

Louie Giglio, founder of The Passion
Movement and Passion City Church

"For the last thirty years, Floyd has always been something of a spiritual litmus test for the church, and his prophetic instincts over time have proved true. And Floyd is right again … God is definitely calling us to attend to this most fundamental of facts about the authentic Christian life: what it means to be an *untamed disciple of the wild Jesus.*"

Alan Hirsch, author of *ReJesus* and
Untamed, www.theforgottenways.org

"Floyd McClung has done what seems impossible—he's written a fresh and intriguing book on the basics of discipleship. You'll love this book and want to share it with everyone who is serious about following Jesus and becoming like Him."

Carl Medearis, author of *Muslims, Christians,
and Jesus* and *Tea With Hezbollah*

"Floyd gets it! Disciplemaking is all about Jesus. Where we've used other models, we've failed. When we've come back to the source, we've known revival. This book is all about getting back to the source—in simple and practical ways that can work with anyone, anywhere."

Ralph Moore, author of *How To Multiply Your Church*

"I've been a serious follower of Christ for more than three decades, yet I found something in every chapter of *Follow* that either challenged me, inspired me, or encouraged me—often all three. This book will be required reading in our discipleship training process."

Ron Parrish, director of Hope for the Nations and pastor of Hope in the City

"If you are a committed follower of Jesus or someone who is just beginning to inquire about what that would mean, you should read *Follow.* Beware: It is a radical and life-changing message!"

Jane Overstreet, president and CEO of Development Associates International

"If you are looking for keys to live the kind of life God intended for His children—and to help others do the same—you need look no further. *Follow* is both inspirational and practical. Reading and applying these biblical truths will change your life."

Maureen Menard, vice president for Leadership Equipping with Youth With A Mission

FOLLOW

A Simple and Profound Call
to Live Like Jesus

F L O Y D   M c C L U N G

David C Cook®
transforming lives together

FOLLOW
Published by David C. Cook
4050 Lee Vance View
Colorado Springs, CO 80918 U.S.A.

David C. Cook Distribution Canada
55 Woodslee Avenue, Paris, Ontario, Canada N3L 3E5

David C. Cook U.K., Kingsway Communications
Eastbourne, East Sussex BN23 6NT, England

The Web site addresses recommended throughout this book are offered as a resource to you. These Web sites are not intended in any way to be or imply an endorsement on the part of David C. Cook, nor do we vouch for their content.

LCCN 2010928373
ISBN 978-1-4347-0192-3
eISBN 978-1-4347-0251-7

© 2010 Floyd McClung, Jr.
First edition published as *Following Jesus* by Struik Christian Media
in 2009 © Floyd McClung, ISBN 978-1-4153-0747-2.

The Team: Richard Herkes, Amy Kiechlin, Sarah Schultz, Caitlyn York, Karen Athen
Cover design: SurfaceWorks Design, Mark Ross
Cover images: iStockphoto, royalty-free

Printed in the United States of America
Second Edition 2010

1 2 3 4 5 6 7 8 9 10

053110

To Sally,
who keeps on following Jesus,
first to Afghanistan, then Amsterdam, and now Africa

Contents

Foreword

As a college student, I found myself standing in my driveway trying to make sense of my newfound faith. As I prayed and asked God to help me understand, immediately the clear teaching of Jesus came to mind: "If you love Me with all your soul, mind, and strength, and love your neighbor as yourself, in this is the fullness of the law." While all the teachings of Jesus were wrapped up in these basic truths, I realized that if I would simply pursue loving Jesus every day with all my heart, if I would compassionately reach out in love to others, whether they were followers of Jesus or absolutely opposed to Him, then this law of love would change the world. This law of love would be powerful enough to heal hearts, to heal families, to restore nations, and to see the gospel of the kingdom proclaimed in all the earth.

Along the way, God has brought men and women into my life to mentor and to teach me how to engage the heart of God and to heal the hearts of people. Floyd McClung is one of those mentors. From his earliest days of ministry in Afghanistan, to the streets of Amsterdam, to churches in America, and now in his current location in South Africa, Floyd has lived out this biblical admonition.

In *Follow* you will not only find biblical truth to back up these basic values that change the world, but you will find a life that has been lived in accordance with these basic values.

Follow is not simply a set group of truths but a life to be lived. When that life is lived well, there is not only joy but fruitfulness in every direction. In this book you will find profound insight from the Word of God together with practical tools in how to live that abundant life that Christ has promised to us. I know that Floyd's desire has always been to change the world. He and his wife, Sally, have not only impacted my family, but they have also impacted thousands of others. Amazingly enough, this impact has not just been because of their great dreams and visions and anointed teaching and preaching, but through living from the inside out, embodying a life of love, working that out in their day-to-day life and therefore having an incredible inheritance both in this life and in the one to come.

Thanks, Floyd and Sally, for the way you have lived your lives; for the way you have stayed true to the gospel, to the good news that Jesus loves us, that He loves everyone around us, and that He longs to change the world through us.

Jimmy Seibert
Antioch Community Church
Waco, Texas

INTRODUCTION

Simple Yet Profound

All followers and seekers of Jesus must wrestle with three simple yet profound truths. Worship. Mission. Community. They are simple, but they will affect every area of your life if you allow them to. Once again, they are:

1. Worship: to love and obey Jesus as a lifestyle—with passion and purpose.
2. Mission: to love those who don't follow Jesus—with courage and decency.
3. Community: to love other followers of Jesus—with intentionality and transparency.

Disciple was the preferred word of Jesus' day for students of a Jewish rabbi or priest. It was also the word most often used to describe those who were closest to Jesus. The Greek word for disciple is *mathetes*, which means a "taught" or "trained" person.[1] Some of Jesus' disciples followed Him out of curiosity, others for selfish reasons. Many left Him altogether when He asked of them more than they were willing to give. But, for those who remained with Him, theirs was the privilege of having their world turned upside down by the most radical of all revolutionaries.

For us, as followers and seekers of Jesus, everything that is good and true about us will flow from knowing and being like Jesus. This discovery of true faith in Jesus determines in turn how we convey our faith to others, which will define what kind of community we build with others of similar faith.

To quote Michael Frost and Alan Hirsch in their book *ReJesus*,

> Following Jesus involves more than simply accepting Him as your Savior via some prayer of commitment, no matter how sincere that prayer may be. In order to follow Jesus, you must also emulate him, using his life as a pattern for your own.[2]

I am struck by these words—*using his life as a pattern for your own*. I think all of us—whether seeker or convinced follower—will agree that, if Jesus is indeed God, then to truly follow Him is to pattern *everything* in our lives after His life. That reality forms the backdrop for this book. It is not written to simply inspire, but with the conviction that if Jesus is who He said He is, then following Him should invade every area of our lives and transform everything about us.

If Jesus is indeed God, then to truly follow Him is to pattern *everything* in our lives after His life.

Follow is about the foundation on which we

build our lives—Jesus Himself. The only way we can truly authenticate ourselves as seekers and followers of Jesus is to measure ourselves by the life and teachings of Jesus. Not by our leaders or our doctrinal statements—just Jesus! Not by what church or organization we are part of, but by Jesus Himself. And certainly not by the false "self" that our culture tries to press on us, defined by "what I have" or "what I do." *Just Jesus*.

When Jesus gave birth to the church two thousand years ago, He designed it so that it was intrinsically resistant to institutionalization. The way that Jesus sets for us is

> inherently subversive against all attempts to control, and thus institutionalize, the revelation that he so powerfully ushers in. In other words, it's just plain hard to create a religion out of the way of Jesus.[3]

I have written this book with the underlying belief that *any* hierarchy and *all* institutionalization of the church lead us directly away from Jesus Himself. We must, therefore, constantly return to Jesus as our source and our example for how to live life and how to do church together. Studying His life, spending time in His presence, seeking to be filled with His Spirit, and fulfilling His mission with others in community—this is how we are to experience life as Jesus intended it.

I write, too, with the underlying belief that Jesus will bypass and resist all attempts to domesticate and tame Him! We cannot franchise Jesus. We cannot reduce Him to a method or a model. None of us should ever attempt to be Jesus for other people. We are on dangerous ground when we do. If Jesus bypassed the religious leaders of His day because they tried to capture God for other people, He will not be reluctant to do the same today to Christian leaders.

It is not easy to have a clear vision of the true Jesus, "particularly when you live with a culture that is far askew"[4] from His way. I grew up in a church culture that embraced racism. We were an all-white denomination begun in the Deep South in the United States. It took the speeches and civil disobedience of Martin Luther King Jr. to awaken my conscience to the evil of racism during my time as a searching university student. It was only then I realized that I had inherited a Christian culture I had mistaken for the teachings and practices of Jesus. King's message of nonviolence in the face of injustice inspired me to dream a bigger dream of what it meant to follow Jesus.

We cannot franchise Jesus. We cannot reduce Him to a method or a model.

It is very hard to find Jesus when you live within a culture that claims to be Christian but is far from the Jesus way. At present I live in Cape Town, South Africa. I visited South Africa many times during the apartheid years. White South Africans in those days claimed to have built a Christian nation. It was enshrined in their constitution. Many South Africans naively trusted the propaganda of the National Party, which ruled the country. Instead of applying the radical teachings of Jesus to the racist doctrines of apartheid, they blindly trusted their leaders to think for them. It is a hard lesson to learn, whether in South Africa, Nazi Germany, the United States, or the United Kingdom.

We learn from Jesus' example while on earth that He did not come to set up "Christian nations." Jesus modeled being an underking. His kingdom was not married to any political party or country. We learn from this that we must continually go back to Jesus and His example of "subversive resistance" to all that is contrary to His way. We must study His teachings, look deeply at His example, and ask hard questions of ourselves and others about what it means to follow Jesus. This applies to Republicans and Democrats in the United States, Tories and Labour in the UK, any and all political parties and philosophies.

I seek to ask hard questions of you in this book, questions of what you believe and how you apply those beliefs to your everyday life. I have tried to put aside my own assumptions as I consider again what it means to follow Jesus, and I ask you to do the same. I fully acknowledge that no one can ever claim to understand or know Jesus completely, but we can know Him with certainty. Not with arrogant self-certainty, but with confident humility.

This book describes in some detail the three most basic truths of those who follow Jesus and shows how to nurture those truths so they are in alignment with how you live. In other words, *Follow* is about how to be a fully devoted disciple of Jesus and not a pretender or an unthinking captive to cultural Christianity. It attempts to describe both the cost of discipleship and the beauty of living the Jesus way.

The three basic truths of discipleship we stated at the beginning of this introduction are, in one way, simple: to love Jesus, to love the world the way Jesus loves it, and to love others who love Jesus.

Worship—Love Jesus.

Mission—Love the world.

Community—Love one another.

Very simple. But building one's life on these three simple yet profound truths goes deeper than a first glance reveals. They might be simple, but they are not easy. They are approachable and touchable, but once you get close to them, they demand your whole life. By their nature you cannot pay lip service to them and then carry on, life as usual, on your own terms. By engaging these three basic truths of discipleship, we discover what it means to love authentically. We become what Dietrich Bonhoeffer refers to as "people for others."

Nothing that is profoundly true—even though it might appear simple on the surface—comes without paying a price. The price for Jesus was the cross. The cross cost God His Son and Jesus His life. And if it cost Jesus His life, it will cost His followers their lives as well. Not always their physical lives, but certainly the right to control their lives selfishly.

Becoming Like Jesus—*For the Sake of Others*

As those who follow Jesus, we are people for others. Being a fully devoted follower of Jesus is about something bigger than what *I* believe and how *I* live; it is about far more than us as individual, private persons. Following Jesus is personal—but it is not private! Some Christians—in fact, many so-called followers of Jesus—mistakenly believe that the Christian life is about what they personally believe to be true in the privacy of their own hearts, and then living those beliefs the way they privately interpret them. But there is much more to this life than a private endeavor. Much more is at stake.

Following Jesus is not a private matter. It is not for you to work out on your own, for yourself and by yourself. If you choose to follow

Jesus, to commit or recommit your life to Him, then you can do so on His terms but not your own.

You are part of God's people if you follow Jesus. And God's people are in this world for God and others, not themselves. We are His family. We are part of a multicultural, global community, each one working out a personal-not-private faith in community with others and for others.

Jesus did not come just to reward us with a private kind of faith—as appealing as that may be to some people. Serving Jesus is not just about our personal lifestyle and beliefs. Being a disciple of Jesus is about conforming our lives to the grander story of His life and purpose on the earth—together with other followers of Jesus.

Jesus came to turn the world upside down. Evil might rule the world for now, and corrupt dictators might have their day, but those on top will someday find themselves upended by the true King. Jesus sees and feels the injustice of those exploited by human trafficking. He hears the cries of the single mother and the battered housewife. He agonizes over the hopelessness of the poor. He is angry over war and economic injustice. He turned over the tables of the money changers in the temple two thousand years ago, and He is busy doing the same today, through those who follow Him.

Jesus came to earth not just to save us personally with a private kind of salvation; He came to establish His radical, sweeping, upending kingdom on earth. Salvation is more than praying a private prayer to accept Jesus and then carrying on living for ourselves—life as it always was but now with some "eternal-life insurance" thrown in. Jesus came to establish His rule on earth. It is a kingdom of the heart, but He is working toward a global revolution. He came to create a new community of followers who will live passionately for Him and carry out His purposes on the earth. This is the kingdom of God, which He spoke about so often. Jesus living on *in* us as the ruler and King of our lives—and *through* us transforming the world.

What God made in the garden when He created Adam and Eve was marred by the worst kind of selfishness. It was rebellion in the face of goodness. When God came in human form much later as Jesus, He came to remake and restore what He started in the garden, to begin the extreme process of eliminating the selfishness that entered and destroyed His planet. Creation groans under the weight of exploitation and selfishness—it awaits its day of liberation. All of creation, each of us, suffers from the impact of sin. That is why we need a radical makeover of the heart and lifestyle. It's the reason we need a Savior.

And it is why we must reform our worldview and philosophy of life. We are called to live by His script, not ours. To help you do just that, let's start at the beginning; let's start with His story, and, if you are willing, take up your part in the story.

So first: God's Story ...

PROLOGUE

God's Story

Episode 1—Creation

The Story begins long before there was time, color, or any living thing; before the stars were made; before the dinosaurs roamed the earth. The Great One chose to use His creative powers to speak our planet into existence, to fill it with animals and plants and rivers and mountains. Great One made the trees, rocks, rivers, and animals, but He was different from them. He did not use His power because He was forced to do so, or because He lacked anything in Himself, but because He wanted to create beauty and share it with others.

In His crowning achievement, Great One made Man and Woman, limited in power and knowledge but astonishing in beauty and creativity. They were like Great One, but they were no match for Him. Great One named them, gave them a home, and visited them each evening to converse with them and enjoy their pleasure as they named and interacted with His creation. Great One created Man and Woman to share with Him in friendship and community and to be partners with Him in loving and caring for His creation.

Episode 2—Rebellion

A great Rebellion started in Great One's home. Unfathomably, Beautiful Creatures made by Great One decided to attempt to overthrow Him. Their Rebellion failed, and a third were driven away from Great One's presence. One of them visited Man and Woman. He deceived them, and they, too, joined the great Rebellion.

When Great One came for His evening visit with Man and Woman, they were missing. He could not find them. Loneliness was tangible, and sadness hung in the air. "Where are you?" He shouted tearfully. "I miss you…. Why have you left Me?"

Man and Woman were hiding. When Great One found them, their faces were covered with shame and their bodies draped with strange garments. Man and Woman had always been so at ease in the presence of Great One. But now they were ashamed. This was the shattering consequence of their Rebellion.

Great One sent Man and Woman from their home, pronouncing judgment on them for their betrayal. They had joined the Rebellion and broken friendship and trust with Great One. Their separation from Great One was a living death to them. The death infected their descendants and all of creation like a strange and alien virus.

Episode 3—Sacrifice

The next episode in the Story is about Sacrifice, which is when someone gives up something of great value for somebody else. Great One longed for Man and Woman to return, but they persisted in their Rebellion, followed by their offspring. Anger and violence filled Great One's creation. Great One sent messengers, entreating everyone to turn away from the Rebellion. But they rejected the messengers.

Finally, Great One chose to visit Man and Woman once again. Perhaps if He came to them in person they would listen, change their minds, resign from their foolish ways and return to their Creator.

Great One had conceived a Plan long before, His greatest and final effort to win back Woman and Man; and He was now ready to carry it out. He used His creative powers to become like Man and Woman, to come close to them in kindness and in strong weakness, to speak to them so they could understand. Surely, Great One reasoned, if He became LikeMan-LikeWoman, they would listen to Him.

Great One longed to say that He missed them, that He yearned for them to return. But He would not be true to Himself if He ignored their Rebellion and accepted them back without their remorse.

To His great sadness, Man and Woman turned on LikeMan-LikeWoman. They blamed Him for all the problems they had brought upon themselves. Their guilt spilled out in rage. Instead of remorse, they chose blame. So they killed LikeMan-LikeWoman. They mocked Him. Tortured Him. Abused Him. Scorned Him. And killed Him.

Episode 4—Return

But death could not hold the One who created life. Great One startled Woman and Man by appearing to them after the Sacrifice. He announced that He would turn their act of hatred and rejection into His way of forgiving them. Instead of punishing them, He would use His death to offer them forgiveness. The death of LikeMan-LikeWoman would be substitution for the punishment they deserved. If they would return to Him, acknowledge Great One, and leave the Rebellion, He would forgive them. Although they deserved to die, He would take their punishment. Amazingly, He chose to use their act of ultimate Rebellion to be His act of ultimate Forgiveness.

Episode 5—Commission

Some of Man and Woman's descendants returned to Great One, asking forgiveness for their part in the Rebellion. To their astonishment, Great One explained that He not only forgave them but commissioned them to be Story-Tellers, to join Great One in telling His Story by telling their part in the Story. This was the Fulfillment of what Great One had begun in the beginning. Man and Woman would share in intimacy and purpose with Great One and would live their part of Great One's Story.

And so the Story was told far and wide. Some sang the Story, some wrote it in parables, and others lived it among those too poor to read the Story for themselves. And in telling the Story, the Story-Tellers found Fulfillment. What they had sought but never found in the Rebellion, they enjoyed naturally in friendship with Great One as they lived their part in the Story. They discovered that what had been lost in the days of the Rebellion was now restored to them.

The Story Continues …

There is a last episode in the Story, but it is still being written. Great One only smiles and nods His head when asked how the Story ends. Though the Rebellion continues, Great One has declared victory.

And that brings us to *your* part in the Story. You do have a part in God's Story. Each of us does. God's Story won't be complete without you.

Part One

LOVING JESUS

ONE

Repenting of Religion

I want you to imagine what my reaction would have been, when I wrote to Sally (now my wife), asking her to marry me, if her response had been as follows:

Dear Floyd,

I would love to marry you. It's a dream come true! The answer is YES!

There are a few minor details, though. I have a couple of other boyfriends—well, seven to be exact. Most of them don't mean much to me, but can I keep Murray and Wayne? I must be in love, because I've never before been willing to give up so many of my boyfriends! My mother says you're a lucky man!

There's one other thing. I will accept your proposal on the condition that I can stay in Texas and live with my parents. I love them. They have done so much for me that I couldn't dream of leaving them. You wouldn't want me to hurt their feelings, would you? However, you can visit

whenever you want to. I'm sure you understand. Oh, and

one last thing … I don't want to upset you, but I would

prefer not to take your name. McClung is just not that

pretty a name.

I look forward to setting the wedding date!

Yours in undying love and devotion,

Sally

Had I received that kind of reply from Sally to my marriage proposal, I would have run the other way. In truth, I pursued Sally with late-night phone calls, visits to Texas to see her, and long letters sharing my desires for our future together, hoping that she would share those dreams. I pursued Sally because I loved her. I was convinced she was the woman for me. When I finally did ask Sally to marry me, I expected that if she loved me and she was "the one," she would lay aside all others for me. And so she did—"McClung" name and all! She was smitten with me, and I with her!

That's what true love is—committing to love another person. We would feel cheated by any other kind of relationship.

In the same way, God pursues us because He loves us, to remind us that He loves us, all to draw us back to Himself. Sending Jesus was

My story is not about how I *found* religion, but how I was *set free from* religion.

the most visible expression of this. Jesus is God's way of romancing us. Just as I courted and pursued Sally, so, in a much more profound way, God pursues each of us.

My Story

I realized a long time ago that we all have a God Story to tell, a story
of how God radically transformed us through faith in Jesus. Our
story finds its full meaning in God's Story.

My story is not about how I *found* religion, but how I was *set
free from* religion. I didn't have to repent of sin as much as I had to
repent of the sin of religion. For me, religion was about powerful
people controlling my life and others' lives. Maybe some of those
powerful people were sincere, but they had strayed far from loving
people Jesus' way. And the sad thing about it was that I became like
those powerful people. But let me tell the story from the beginning.

Before Jesus

I grew up with Christian religion. Someone could make a Hollywood
movie of my life, it was so weird. We were wild-eyed fundamentalists. We attended church meetings up to five times a week: prayer
meetings, revival meetings, midweek meetings, youth meetings,
and, of course, two Sunday meetings. There was a lot of sincere zeal,
but people lived inside a religious bubble of meetings and so-called
Christian culture.

When I was a teenager, people's hypocrisy made me cynical about
my religion. Many people in church professed one thing but lived
another. There were lots of rules but not much love. I tried to fit in, but
the journey, filled with my insecurity and zeal to perform, was hard.

My parents were good people. In fact, my father was a pastor,
a saintly man, deeply religious in the best sense of that word. He
prayed by the hour, loved impossible people, and gave his life to
being a "good shepherd." But I struggled with others in our church.

One of the most difficult parts of my church experience was how judgmental people were. They passed judgment on the clothes people wore, the things they did or didn't do for God, and whether they kept the church's rules for "holy living." Holy was not defined by how loving you were but by how extreme you were. But in my later teen years, that same religious attitude crept into my own heart. What I despised, I became.

Growing up with religion made me feel like a failure. I lived with feelings of false guilt—though at the time I didn't know the guilt was false! I continually felt a sense of shame and tried to prove myself worthy of the church's blessing. I hid my sins and weaknesses from others in the church, while I sought their approval and acceptance.

How God's Love Became Real to Me

One of the best things that happened to me was going to university. I loved sports, which became an important part of my life. I achieved success, as well as a fair bit of notoriety, and my self-confidence grew. I became the captain of our basketball team, and we traveled the country, defeating teams from universities ten and twenty times our size. Newspapers across the United States wrote about us. Professional scouts from the NBA came to watch us play. It was exhilarating. But I was still in turmoil regarding my faith.

During this time, one of my professors had a huge influence on my life. I liked him as a person; he was honest, spent time with the students in the resident halls, attended student activities and sports events I was involved in. He became a role model to me.

This professor was a very devout man but devoid of "religion." This fascinated and intrigued me. At the end of each of his lectures, he would push back his notes, stand up behind his desk, and speak to us from his heart. He pleaded with us to be people who would change the world. He spoke passionately about being free from the chains of religion. He invited us to be fully human and fully alive.

One day, he spoke about the difference between religion and God's love. He told us the difference between performing and living our lives from the heart—and I realized that up to that point I had lived to please people; but that was not what God wanted from me, nor did it somehow persuade God to love me. As my professor pleaded with us to be free from religion and alive with the grace and love of God, a light went on in my heart. In my inner person I agreed, and I walked out of the class a free man. I realized that I had been taught most of my life that devotion was *duty* to God, not *delight* in God. I quietly determined to live for delight, not duty.

The Change *Jesus* Made in My Life

As a result of that inner transaction, the weight of religion with rules rolled off me like a heavy backpack falling to the ground. Who took it and how it was lifted off me, I wasn't sure, but it was gone. I felt free. I knew from that moment, I didn't need to do anything— indeed could not do anything—to *make* God love me. I didn't have to do things to earn God's love. I was free to love God simply because He loved me first. I felt light, free, and full of hope.

Since that day, I have lived like a man unshackled from prison chains. I live like an orphan who has been adopted into a loving family. I feel fully human, alive, set free to enjoy God. I don't feel alone or that I have to do things to gain the approval of people or of God.

I now wake up every day with a deep sense of God's love and acceptance. I know I belong to God. Being loved by God is incredible! Accepting His love and forgiveness is my response to that incredible love.

Loving God begins with the discovery that He has created us for intimacy and friendship with Him. It is accompanied by a longing to live life to the fullest; to see and taste and hear all life has for us. God has adventure waiting for us, beauty to share with us, dreams and purpose and security and significance to give to us.

What Does It Mean to Love Jesus?

Our theme in the first part of this book is *loving Jesus*. I know, and I hope you know as well, that loving Jesus is a heart response to His love for us, involving a commitment to obey Jesus each day of our lives. But we must allow God to love us to the point where He captures our *complete* devotion.

To be captured by Jesus is to be captivated by Him, fascinated and intrigued with who He is and what He has in store for us. Loving Jesus means opening our hearts to Him, holding back nothing, confessing everything—our weaknesses and fears, dreams and longings.

Loving Jesus has to be lived out in the face of constant temptation to conform and compromise. This pressure can come from myriad sources: from the influence of our culture and its more depraved and dehumanizing demands, to the more naive, but sometimes painful, interactions with friends and family. It can come from people we work with or go to school with, and from movies, TV, and certain types of music. Jesus wants to give us the strength to withstand the pressures contrary to His way so that we can live our lives for Him and His purposes.

We're all slaves to something or someone—either willing love slaves or unwilling slaves to private prisons we make. We were created to be fully devoted to God, and if we're not fully devoted to God, we'll give that devotion to someone or something else.

Paul the apostle speaks to the Roman believers of this capacity for devotion: "You know well enough from your own experience that there are some acts of so-called freedom that destroy freedom. Offer yourselves to sin, for instance, and it's your last free act. But offer yourselves to the ways of God and the freedom never quits" (Rom. 6:16 MSG). We cannot serve two masters.

We serve the one we love, and we love the one we serve. When we allow Him to love us, we unshackle our hearts to love Him back. This is good news to religious people who want to be free of religion!

We don't behave differently *in order to* be loved by God, but *because* we are loved by God.

Paul goes on to say these incredible words about the love of God:

For all who put their trust in God are children of God. As a result you are set free from acting like fearful, beaten slaves. You should believe and behave instead like God's very own adopted children, loved and accepted into His family. You can freely call out to Him, "Dear Father." And know this with certainty: The Father has sent the Holy Spirit to speak to you deep in your heart—and He keeps on speaking to you until you finally believe

it—that you are God's loved children. (Rom. 8:14–16,
author's paraphrase)

Though we were once slaves to our passions, desires, fears, and hurts, we are set free to love God with our whole hearts. No longer do we have to be prisoners. This is the good news of the gospel!

God's love invades our minds, changing our core values and transforming our behavior. We don't behave differently *in order to* be loved by God, but *because* we are loved by God. We realize that God is not trying to punish us for our past sins but deliver us from them. He is not out to heap shame on us for past failures but to take our shame away and give us the great gift of finally, fully belonging.

What Hinders Us from Loving Jesus?

Nothing hinders us from receiving the love of God as much as the lies that build up in our minds about who God is or who we are. Paul describes these lies as "strongholds" in our minds, like fortresses where debilitating accusations wage war against us. A friend of mine describes these lies as the script we try to live by, but a script that is not the "real us." We learn this script from our upbringing, our culture, and painful experiences in life. Our scripts get lodged in our hearts despite what we believe in our minds, becoming a deafening cry of the false self—*what matters most is what I have, what I do, and what others think of me*—instead of the stunning truth that *God likes me; He loves me and unconditionally accepts me.*

The Bible tells us that we must fight to hold on to the truth; we mustn't be passive about these lies: "We are human, but we don't wage war with human plans and methods. We use God's mighty weapons, not mere worldly weapons, to knock down the Devil's strongholds. With these weapons we break down every proud argument that keeps people from knowing God. With these weapons we conquer their rebellious ideas, and we teach them to obey Christ" (2 Cor. 10:3–5 NLT).

You can tell when you believe lies about yourself or God, because they produce hopelessness and mistrust. God sent His Son, Jesus, to die on the cross for our sins and free us from these lies. That great act of redemption provides the power we need to be free from the false self, to be the person God created us to be. We must resist the lies, receive God's love in Jesus, stand for what is true—and forgive those who have communicated those lies to us and about us. There is great power in forgiving and taking responsibility for our feelings and choices. In fighting for truth, we become strong. We overcome passivity and fear and anger and hate. It is not easy, but fighting to take hold of the love of God is well worth the battle.

To love Jesus and allow Him to love us is to fight for what we know in our minds to be true. In doing this, we allow the doctrinal beliefs we know to be intellectually true to become deeply *real* to us, to go deep into our hearts. It is then that the love of God in Jesus transforms us. Believing in Jesus is not just a nice religious thing to do. Integrating that belief into the deepest part of our being transforms every aspect of our lives.

The Price of Being Free

You can be free to love God with your whole being, as a whole, passionate, free person. And in doing so, you are freed to become intensely aware of being loved by God. Loving God unlocks your heart and frees you to live above your fears.

But there is a price to pay. God invites us to turn away from lesser pleasures as our source of meaning and purpose to the ultimate pleasure of knowing and loving Him.

Jesus told a parable of a man who went to build a tower but did not have enough money to complete it. He said the man, to save embarrassment and wasted effort, should have sat down and calculated the cost before starting. "So therefore," Jesus says, "whoever of you does not renounce all that he has cannot be my disciple" (Luke 14:33 RSV).

Those who are considering becoming, or are already committed to being, fully devoted followers of Jesus must count the cost of putting Him first in their lives. That doesn't mean renouncing who He created you to be, but renouncing the false beliefs and behaviors that have kept you from being *all* He created you to be.

What Loving Jesus Does *Not* Mean

In order to grasp what it means to love Jesus, we need to consider what it does *not* mean.

Becoming a "religious" freak

Loving God does not mean that God expects you to become religious or speak "Christianese." My friend David, full of newfound faith and enthusiasm for Jesus, joined a church and was immediately handed a set of regulations covering everything from where he could go and when, how long his hair could be, and even with whom he could associate. Tragically, the rule book dealt with everything except what mattered most—a heart of devotion to Jesus, which can't be reduced to a set of rules. The implication of the rule-book approach to spirituality is that it can produce conformity without pleasure, zeal without genuine maturity. Sometimes, zeal lacks depth and produces so-called model Christians who are plastic imitations of the real thing. Some religious leaders fear or resent this perspective, but maybe that's because they can't control people without it.

Jesus spoke scathingly of the religious leaders of His day because they had reduced a relationship with God to a set of detailed and often ridiculous regulations. Yet some Christian leaders today unfortunately think in the same way. Their way of making people "holy" is to load them down with a long list of dos and don'ts or a strict conformity to their definition of spirituality. This approach, however, only produces fear, dependence, and condemnation. The more control and rules there are, the greater our sense of failure when we are unable to please our earthly leaders. Looking back at my time as a brash young leader who demanded that type of loyalty, I now realize how detrimental my actions were to people's delight in God. I tried too hard, and as a result, I got in the way. The older I am the more I realize that my role is to stay in the background.

The kind of devotion that God delights in comes about when a person finds security in the pure, unselfish love of God. We don't find our security or our value from the rules we obey or the way we live. But in the love of God, we know that there is nothing we can do to make Him love us more or less—He just loves us!

Performing to earn approval

There is safety in knowing we are "okay" with everyone. Many followers of Jesus try to find security in living up to the expectations of others—the silent code of conduct a group has for itself. There is security in conforming. It means we think we are loved, or okay with God, because we are okay with people. However, God doesn't grade us according to how good our performance is or by whether we have performed certain religious duties or not. He has offered up His Son Jesus as a substitute sacrifice for our sins, as the means by which we are acceptable to Him. No amount of trying to gain His approval by doing our duty or conforming to some man-made code will ever change that great truth.

Temptations will go away

Even once we accept Jesus' acceptance, we will be tempted to go back to the old way of trying to earn His love or indulging ourselves in the short-lived pleasures of sin. Whether the sorts of temptations you face are to lust, lie, steal, or fall back on "good behavior," Jesus made it clear that we will face temptations of both a religious and nonreligious type. Jesus Himself was tempted and did not sin, which means we can be tempted—without sinning. Temptation to sin is not sin, although we often think it is. It can sometimes be confusing to know the difference as we wrestle with inner thoughts and feelings.

Jesus was tempted in the wilderness by the Devil, yet He was without sin. He was tempted, just as we are, when Satan presented Him with thoughts of power, wealth, recognition—shortcuts to becoming all the Father wanted Him to be. But He did not give in to temptation. He did not leave the wilderness with feelings of defeat and unworthiness.

If you struggle to discern the difference between temptation and sin, then be direct with God and ask Him, "Have I sinned? What specifically did I do wrong, and how can I correct it?" God is committed to helping us lead lives of truthfulness. He will show us the difference between sin and the temptation to sin.

If, after talking to God about this, nothing comes to mind, then quite possibly you are dealing with vague accusations of sin or suffering from false guilt that religious people want to pile on you. If you are feeling powerless and joyless, go to a mature Christian and pray together. Shake off false guilt and refuse to accept it!

When we are convicted of sin by the Holy Spirit, it will be absolutely clear to us what we have done wrong. Condemnation is vague and related to a general sense of failure rather than to a specific sin; shame is a negative emotion that combines feelings of embarrassment and worthlessness; false-guilt feelings are based on demands from people, not from God, in order to try to control us.

But when the Holy Spirit convicts us of sin, we understand God's grace and the hope that belongs to those who are loved unconditionally by God. Real guilt shows us that we have done wrong and brings us to Jesus. God convicts us of sin because He loves us and wants to help us be free from sin!

The Bible teaches us to resist the Devil so that he will flee from us. If we are tempted and actively resist, then we are not sinning. But when we welcome temptation, entertain it, and give in to it, we have entered into sin.

What Loving Jesus *Does* Mean

We have a purpose to live for!

The world waits for us to bring hope to the poor and freedom to the oppressed. Get involved! God has given you abilities and passions and talents to make a difference in the world. Enjoy your passions and interests—but don't live for them. God has more for you!

We are forgiven!

Jesus' death on the cross is God's way of providing for our forgiveness. When we acknowledge our need of forgiveness, He forgives us—and He does that because of His great love for us.

We are freed from fear!

Loving Jesus means that we allow God to work deeply in our hearts, right down to the level of our secret fears. Fear can be a temptation, or it can be sin. For example, it is natural not to want to be a victim of violent crime, but that doesn't mean we have to live in constant fear. Jesus' teaching on forgiveness and His example of facing and overcoming the cross assure us that we, too, can live in freedom from fear.

We have hope!

God has not abandoned fallen humanity but has come near to us in Jesus. God has provided a wonderful means of redemption, reconciliation, and forgiveness through His Son. Because of the death and subsequent resurrection of Jesus Christ, we need no longer be enslaved to sin or dominated by the fears and worries of daily life. This audacious hope impacts all three tenses of our lives: hope for our past—we are forgiven; hope for our present—Jesus is always with us no matter what; hope for our future—the promise of new life through the resurrection.

We get to serve the poor!

There are people around you without hope. Many are in the grip of financial poverty and others are enslaved to poverty of spirit. You have an answer for them. Get involved. Listen to their stories. Share your God Story with them. Serve them practically.

We have faith to face difficult circumstances!

There is nothing we face that Jesus has not already faced. He was both a Jew and a Palestinian. He knew racial prejudice. He was the victim of crime. He lived under a ruthless foreign power. He was born to an unwed mother. He worked to support His family. Jesus faced temptation. He understands our struggles; He lived through them and conquered them. We will not always be free from fears or feelings of personal rejection or other consequences of living with economic challenges or personal struggles, but Jesus will help us win the battle.

You write God's Story through your life. You add to God's Story. Your choices, your responses to the love of God, are important to Him. You show the love of God every day to others. As you accept His love and forgiveness for you, you bring hope to others by your example. You are making the God Story real to others, "acted" out on the stage of your life. God is the director, He is in the drama, and we already know the final scene. We have read the last chapter, so we know who wins in the end!

Reflecting and Responding

1. **Read and reflect on Romans 8:14–16.**

2. **Write out your personal story in three parts:**
   - What your life was like before you experienced the forgiving love of God in Jesus
   - How God's love through Jesus became real to you
   - What difference the love of God in Jesus has made in your life

If you are "still on the journey," write about where you are now in your search for God's love. Use less than three hundred words. Then share it with a few friends and other followers of Jesus.

3. **How can pressure from family, friends, coworkers, and movies/television/music tempt us away from loving Jesus? List those pressures.**

4. **What "lies" are you tempted to tell yourself that can be barriers between you and the love of God?**

TWO

Obedience

Once we give our lives completely to God, the first question we often ask is, "What does He want me to do with my life?" Or more commonly, "How do I know God's will for my life? Is God sending me to Africa? Yikes! How can He do that to me?"

The answer is found in a simple yet profoundly challenging commitment: Make it your purpose to obey God's will for your life no matter what He asks of you, sight unseen.

Many Christ followers get caught up in the personal aspects of obedience and forget the main thing: Unconditional surrender to a loving God comes naturally to those in love with Jesus. They worry about whether they will like what God wants them to do and forget that obedience to God is an act of gratitude, not servitude. They tend to get lost in the "what, when, and where," while Jesus sees the big picture. His main concern is our joyful willingness to obey Him.

When we are focused on what we like or don't like, we grow distant from God and His passionate purposes for the earth. God has much more in mind than making us happy. I know it doesn't seem as if there could be anything more important than the person you will marry, or the right career choices, or where you will live, but believe me, a few other things are more important. The answers to the big questions about your life's direction are part of the details of obedience, but they are not the *heart* of obedience. What God has in mind is not hard to discover if you are committed to obedience. He is able to reveal His will for your life to you, no question. But do you want to know the will of God for your life so you can decide if you like it or not? Or do you want to know so you can please God and obey Him?

This is the heart of obedience. Why do we want to know more from God? To negotiate with Him? Do you tend to say to God, "I'll give You such and such if You do so and so for me"? Or are you prepared

The greater our effort to recover the divine image and the prouder we become of that effort, the further we actually remove ourselves from our Creator.

to commit to obey His will, even without knowing what it is?

In the prologue, "God's Story," we were reminded that, after Great One created Woman and Man, there was a cosmic Rebellion against Him. That Rebellion boils down to one word: *disobedience.* Disobedience comes from a proud heart that thinks it knows best. Adam and Eve disobeyed what God had made clear. It was not complicated. It came down to trust in God's goodness.

As a consequence, Adam and Eve experienced severe discord with God. And we as human beings have all made the same insane choice, one person after another. In our unspoiled created state we were like God, but that has been lost. It was lost because of the

Rebellion, because of prideful disobedience. We chose not to trust that God knows what is best for us (Rom. 5:12).

Through the Rebellion (what most theologians term the fall, but let's call it what it is) we lost the ability to live as fully alive, fully human people. Spiritual death became more of a reality than life. The list of global woes bears sad witness to death at work: wars, abuse, human trafficking, rape, poverty, corruption, greed. In this reality of spiritual death, we face the paradox of our existence and the source of our pain and alienation. We are alive physically but dead spiritually without God. Death is at work in us because we have rebelled against our Creator.

Since the Rebellion took its terrible toll, we have striven to recover our God-likeness. Yet paradoxically, the greater our efforts to remake ourselves without God, the greater our separation from God becomes. The greater our effort to recover the divine image and the prouder we become of that effort, the further we actually remove ourselves from our Creator. We don't realize this, but that's because deception always follows disobedience.

The image of God in us became misshapen and marred through rebellion. The more we model our lives on gods of our own invention, the less human and alive we become. The further we grow away from God, the more we become like the Beautiful Creature, Satan, the one who led the first Rebellion against God in heaven.

But Great One has not left us in our lostness. As Dietrich Bonhoeffer wrote, God's plans are to "recover His first delight in His handiwork."[1] Bonhoeffer continued:

> There is only one way to achieve this purpose and
> that is for God, out of sheer mercy, to assume the

image and form of fallen man. As man can no longer
be like the image of God, God must become like
the image of man.... It is not enough for man simply to recover right ideas about God, or to obey his
will in isolated actions of his life. No, man must be
re-fashioned as a living whole in the image of God.[2]

God is on a mission to love and restore His fallen world. If this is
God's purpose for every human being, surely this is reason enough for us
as reborn men and women to cooperate with God through obedience?
Surely this is the whole reason to submit to God's will, that we might
recover the very purpose and heart of who we were created to be?

We are formed after a model. So this is our choice: Either we model
ourselves on gods of our own making, or we allow God to mold us into
His image, the very model of which is Jesus. Which will it be for you?

If you are a halfhearted follower of Jesus, you will persist in
choosing when and where and what you will do in order to obey
God. Or will you allow God
to transform you uncondi-
tionally? Obedience is what
God requires if you say yes.
Unconditional obedience.
Obedience because of love.

> Since we cannot remake
> ourselves to be like God
> ... will we allow God to
> remake us to be like Him?

Personal Transformation

Obedience is responding to the love of God. Obedience to God is
gratitude to God for coming to us in the crucified God-Man, Jesus.
Since we cannot remake ourselves to be like God, will we allow God

to remake us to be like Him? There must be a total transformation of who we are, and that requires total love—and total obedience in response to that love. We need to born all over again. Obedience is cooperating with God as He does that very thing in us.

When I speak of obedience, I don't mean church attendance or refusing to tithe 10 percent or other religious things. Something much more profound is at stake. The issue to settle is this: Will I obey God, period? This a deeply profound choice: Will I allow God to work His will in me so that I might recover what has been lost through my sin and the sins done against me?

The transformation that we cannot bring about in ourselves takes place in and through Jesus—through His extraordinary obedience in dying on the cross. I'm not speaking of ordinary transformation, like transforming a house through the renovation of one room. I am speaking of an extraordinary transformation: the entire house being torn down and rebuilt. This extraordinary transformation impacts our reason for living and being. It gets to the heart of who we are. Jesus desires to set us free from our hiding places and false comforts, to be who He created us to be through obedience to Him.

To be transformed, an image needs a living, true object. Jesus is both the object and the means of our transformation. He longs to reshape us at the core of our being, to reach deep inside us and break away the veneer of plastic reality we have built. He comes to live His life in us. This is good news!

Doing Good Is Not Enough

It is not enough for us to have a good philosophy of life or a better religion to live by in order to be a transformed person. Look how many people—including ourselves—have tried that and failed! Wars still increase despite the best efforts of peacemakers. Selfishness and rebellion abound, as we are reminded again and again through the escapades of renegade bankers and the broken marriages of Hollywood stars. Nations destroy nations. Genocide continues; witness the murders in Rwanda and Darfur or the wars of extermination in Tibet. Political and, yes, religious leaders still play their games of control and manipulation. Fear controls us.

We desperately need the God-Man, Jesus, to come to us as men and women of fallen earth. God has not sent Jesus merely to create in us a new way of thinking or some sort of Christian religious do-goodism but to restore His beautiful image in us.

This obedience is not just doing good deeds; it is allowing God to enter our lives so that our motivations are changed. It is not doing good to be noticed, to fulfill our obligation, to impress others—or even to make ourselves better people. Obedience is capitulation to the love efforts of God to romance us back to Himself, allowing God His rightful place in the deepest parts of our lives, so that our good deeds are based on acknowledging His goodness, not trying to improve our goodness. He could force us, even overwhelm us and make us obey Him, but there would be no love in that.

> **Obedience is capitulation to the love efforts of God to romance us back to Himself.... He could force us, even overwhelm us and make us obey Him, but there would be no love in that.**

The Benefits of Grace-Based Obedience

If we do surrender to Him and embrace obedience to His purposes as a lifestyle, there are many and great benefits that follow.

- Obedience to God makes it possible for us to discover our purpose in life. God sets our destiny, and we discover our destiny by obeying the known will of God (Rom. 12:1–2).

- Obedience gives God great glory and us great satisfaction. The more we find our satisfaction in God, the more He finds His glory in us (Isa. 43:4–7).

- Obedience produces greater intimacy with God. Those who obey Him are closer to Him—they share His wisdom and receive His favor (Isa. 66:2).

- Obedience lays a foundation of godly character in our lives. Those who build their lives on obedience to God have a sure foundation during the storms of life (Matt. 7:24–27).

- Obedience allows God to form Christ in us. By submitting to God's work in us, we become more like Jesus, and the more we become like Jesus, the more we live for the sake of others (Col. 1:21–29).

Extraordinary Obedience, Extraordinary Love

Jesus' love on the cross is so extraordinary that it calls for extraordinary obedience from us. There can be no other response than total surrender. We must invite Him to take control of our lives.

To be transformed to an image of Jesus is not a doctrine to strive for. We cannot transform ourselves to become like Him; it is Jesus who transforms us from within to be like Him, to think and feel and live like Jesus in our flesh.

To become like Jesus means that we are committed to forgive the sins and carry the sorrows of others as Jesus did. We follow Him into a broken, rebellious world to seek and to save those who have lost their way. There is no half way in following Jesus—no following Him yet being unwilling to be part of Jesus changing others. It is all or nothing with Jesus.

Jesus died on a bloody cross, at the hands of those who were part of the rebellion against Him. And fully devoted disciples of Jesus will suffer in a fallen world. We are being conformed to the image of Christ crucified. There is loss. There is rejection. And there will be suffering. Jesus told His disciples He was sending them like lambs among wolves (Luke 10:3). This is the obedience I write about.

This is what I mean when I speak about being transformed to be like Jesus. This is what the Bible speaks about when it declares that Jesus has come to live in our hearts. Jesus continues to live on the earth in the lives of His fully devoted followers. We become part of a "conspiracy of little Jesuses"[3] serving throughout the nations and every sphere of life. As Paul said, "I live, yet it is no longer I who live, but Christ who lives in me" (Gal. 2:20, author's paraphrase). This is what the New Testament speaks about when it speaks of our becoming "like Christ." His life, in and through us, is the life we live.

No man or woman has the right to come between the followers of Jesus and Jesus Himself. The doctrine of extreme submission to an earthly spiritual leader is essentially a false doctrine because we do what we do for Jesus. No mere man deserves this sort of devotion, nor should a leader come between a follower of Jesus and Jesus Himself. Followers of Jesus are to be accountable to one another—true—but not accountable to one leader-person or a small group of leaders who appoint themselves to represent Jesus to the rest of us. Jesus alone is the source of our life and the model for our obedience.

In Genesis 1:26, God gave Adam and Eve dominion over fish, cattle, birds, and "every creeping thing" on the earth (NASB). But He did not give them dominion over people. When spiritual leaders seek to have dominion over people, they exceed God's mandate.

God's mission on earth is to redeem us from our fallen state through servant love (John 3:16). He seeks to win our allegiance through love, not domination. When human leaders seek control out of a misguided sense of spiritual responsibility, they fall into the trap of ruling like an Old Testament king. The people of Israel fell into this trap and ended up with Saul to lead them. God's plea to them was, "Why do you want a king when I will be your King?"

The mission of God is to serve, whereas the mission of fallen humans is to dominate. God wants to restore us to what He created us for: friendship with Him, community with one another, and purpose in life. But the price for us to be part of His mission is the same price Jesus paid: We have to step down from the throne of domination and take up our cross of servanthood.

Jesus has come to live His life in and through us. He is the pattern we follow, and His life is the life we live. John said we are to walk like Jesus (1 John 2:6) and to do as He has done (John 13:15). We are to love as He has loved (Eph. 5:2; John 13:34), forgive as He forgave (Col. 3:13), and have the same lowly attitude He had (Phil. 2:5).[4]

In the New Testament, Peter the apostle tells us we are to follow Jesus' example in suffering: "This is the kind of life you've been invited into, the kind of life Christ lived. He suffered everything that came his way so you would know that it could be done, and also know how to do it, step-by-step" (1 Peter 2:21 MSG).

John the disciple of Jesus tells us we are to lay down our lives in sacrifice and service for our brothers and sisters, just as Jesus did: "This is how we've come to understand and experience love: Christ sacrificed his life for us. This is why we ought to live sacrificially for our fellow believers, and not just be out for ourselves" (1 John 3:16 MSG).

Truths about Grace-Based Obedience

The New Testament reveals certain truths about grace-based obedience. There are not hundreds of "obedience truths," because obedience is simple, though not often easy. These truths should be self-evident to those who are serious about following Jesus:

A response to the love of God revealed in Jesus

Forgiveness and mercy through Jesus are God's way of transforming us. Because He became like us, we can become like Him. Our response to His love is empowered by His grace. What a deal! All that is required on our part is that we say yes to His love. He will not rob us of our freedom to choose to love and serve Him.

A response to the presence of God

God's empowering presence is the work of the Holy Spirit. Experiencing God's presence is not the most important aspect of our relationship with God, but it is a deeply gratifying aspect. It is God's way of drawing us to obedience out of love and gratitude. What we do for God comes not from cold religion but warm relationship.

The fruit of humility and spiritual brokenness

A humble person is one who acknowledges need for God. This gentle state of heart is spiritual "brokenness." Not broken in the sense of beaten down but in the sense of being malleable, open to learn and grow.

An act of gratitude to a merciful God

Our greatest need in life is to be loved by God; the fruit of being loved by Him is obedience from the heart to God.

A lifestyle

If we fail once, that is not the end of the relationship. Learning to trust takes a lifetime of healing and overcoming the lies we have been programmed to believe about ourselves and God. This is a way of life, not a one-off act of religious duty.

Commitment to obeying His will

Understanding the whys of obeying God often follows the act of obeying God. In other words, revelation comes after we obey, not before. God is teaching us to trust who He is, not just what He says, so we don't seek to negotiate over the will of God but ask for strength to obey it.

Love to obey

Obedience involves our will, but most important to God, it involves our heart. When He captures our heart, He knows our choices will follow.

Disciples who make still more disciples

If we don't make disciples, we are not experiencing all God

created us for. God longs for us to experience the joy of having spiritual sons and daughters of our own, people we have brought to faith in Jesus. We are not complete if we don't.

Knowing what Jesus wants us to do

Obedience brings greater revelation of the Father's will for us. God wants us to obey Him with trustful hearts and then teaches us more as we do so. Jesus taught His disciples that the way to stay connected and full of His love was to obey Him. *The Message* says it this way: "If you keep my commands, you'll remain intimately at home in my love. That's what I've done—kept my Father's commands and made myself at home in his love" (John 15:10).

Reflecting and Responding

1. See appendix 1 for instructions on how to do a discovery Bible study, then do a discovery Bible study on Deuteronomy 6:4–9, focusing on heart obedience. What is the one thing God wants of you that you learn in this passage?

2. Why are you interested in knowing God's will?

3. We discussed in this chapter that obedience to God's revealed will is a prerequisite for knowing more of His will. Do you agree or disagree? Explain.

4. What does God's love have to do with obedience?

THREE

Lordship

Loving Jesus means welcoming Him to be Lord of everything in our lives. He made everything and cares about everything He made. If Jesus is God, then pretending to follow Him—and following Him on our own terms—is an insult to Him. To hold back any part of our lives from God is to lend support to the Enemy and take sides in the rebellion of evil against God. That may sound harsh, but think about it this way: He is God. Not a religion or a belief, but the infinite, holy, all-powerful Creator. He deserves nothing less than our absolute surrender to Him. Anything less demeans His greatness.

The nature of true love is commitment. We don't need to be perfect before we can commit our lives fully to Jesus or live sinlessly after we have committed our lives to Him. And we will struggle to give some things over to God's control. But making Jesus the ruler of everything does mean that—to the utmost of my ability and knowledge—we surrender total control of our lives and beliefs to Him.

To ask God to be in control of my life does not mean life will lose its edge. Jesus is not predictable or tame. To echo C. S. Lewis's famous thought in *The Lion, the Witch and the Wardrobe*, He is not a domesticated house cat but a wild lion. He was a threat to the religious establishment of His day—as He will still be today. To quote Alan Hirsch and Michael Frost,

> Jesus was baptized by a wild man. He inaugurated his ministry by spending time with the wild beasts of the wilderness. He was unfazed by a wild storm.... There was an untamed wild power within him.... If your answer to the question "What would Jesus do?" is that he would be conventional, safe, respectable and refined, then we suspect you didn't find that answer in the Gospels.[1]

To be taken captive by the "wildness" of Jesus implies that life will be out of my control, but not out of His control. Every area of my life will be both surrendered to Him and radically reshaped by Him. Everything will be seen in a different light, changing the way I see life, church, God, politics, mission, and the world I live in.

Are you prepared not only to surrender to Him but to rethink your values and beliefs about everything important in life? Making Jesus the Lord of your life means taking time to deliberately reshape how you treat the opposite sex; how you are involved with the poor; how you view work, other races, your politics, everything.

Rethinking and Reshaping

- **Your belief about God Himself**—It is not enough to believe in God. Do you trust Him to be the loving ruler over everything in your life? Do you believe He is good, just, and kind? There are no holy and unholy, spiritual and unspiritual aspects of life to God. Every part of life is either kept for ourselves or submitted to His loving rule. If He rules over our lives, then we do everything as worship to Him. Our choices and attitudes in every aspect of life can be a form of worship to God, or we can divorce God from our everyday lives and limit our understanding of worship to singing a few songs on the "holy day."

- **Your belief about "missions"**—Do you believe some people are called to missions and the rest of us live ordinary lives? If Jesus is the Lord over every part of life—including sports, education, arts, business, and politics—then doesn't Jesus' instruction to pray, "Your kingdom come, Your will be done on earth as it is in heaven …" mean He wants to extend His rule to every part of life? A better word to use, then, than the word *missions,* which may imply that some people do the activity of missions and some do not, is the word *mission.* God does not call just some to be "missionaries," leaving some not called. He is the God of all of life; He has one mission, and that is this: His kingdom ruling over everything! Are you ready to join His mission? If so, He is Lord of your life. And if you are not prepared to serve His mission above your ambitions and plans and preferences, then obviously you are still lord of your life.

- **Your belief about church**—Church is not a templelike building to attend on Sundays, but a community of revolutionary people who make Jesus the Lord of their whole lives and live to accomplish His mission. If Jesus is the Lord of every day and every part of life, and the church is the people who live for His mission, then church happens every day, everywhere! Church is not limited to a holy-day meeting, led by a holy man; it is mission force of radical people invading every vocation and every nation of the world.

Maybe you have been sitting back, criticizing the "church" because you are not willing to be that very church? Making Jesus Lord means you don't wait for the holy man and the holy day; you get on with the job of being a radically obedient disciple of Jesus, making more disciples and gathering with others to read the words of Jesus to learn how to be His obedient followers. Isn't that what believers are doing in the underground church in China? And in the spiritually subversive Jesus movements in the Muslim world? Isn't this what Christ followers are doing as they live among the poor and visit prisons and AIDS hospices? They are listening to Jesus for themselves, then putting into practice what Jesus teaches them to do and be. That is church!

- **Your belief about work**—Because Jesus created all of life and cares about all of life, there are no "unholy" vocations in life. One disciple of mine walked up to me one day with a contagious grin on his face and exclaimed, "I get it! I finally get it! I'm called! What I'm doing is holy! I'm full time." Bruce was a construction foreman who had been waiting for a "call." He thought the highest rung on the "church" ladder of success was to be "called" to be a pastor. Then it finally hit him: He was already called! He got his "calling" when he said yes to Jesus being the Lord of his life. He told me, "My church is my construction crew! I'm the man for them! I'm their pastor!" He went on to tell me how he was discipling the guys on his crew before they were "converted"—discipling them to come to faith, not bringing them to faith to disciple them. He and his wife prayed for his crew, had them in their home, got involved in their marriages, and impacted their lives. When Jesus is the Lord of our lives, being "full time" is not a vocation but an attitude. We say yes to Jesus, and He chooses the location. We embrace our gifts and interests in life, and He mobilizes us to where He wants us to serve Him. Every place is a full-time place of service, and every day is a holy day. Can you see the excitement Bruce experienced, the deep sense of fulfillment he discovered when he realized that church happened as he discipled his guys into faith?

Making Jesus Lord impacts our politics (there are no conservatives or liberals to Jesus, only obedient or disobedient followers, caring or uncaring disciples), our view of creation and the environment, the global economy, the poor—we see everything and everyone from a different perspective when we make Jesus Lord. Many of us are emotionally attached to points of view or activities that may not have anything to do with the kingdom of God. As Christ followers, we must humbly admit we may have mixed-up behaviors and beliefs that may not be what Jesus wants from us. Am I still growing and learning what it means to follow? Or am I one of those Christians who has it all figured out? We have to take the attitude of learners if we are to grow in wisdom and understanding under His lordship.

Lord of Everything!

Being passionate for Jesus is the only passion that will not destroy us. All other passions will take over our lives. By making Him the Lord of our lives, we are protected from being seduced by false beliefs and false pleasures. As we allow the love of Jesus to penetrate our hearts and our minds, we realize that our identity and security come from His love for us and not from our attempts to find meaning in life without Him.

> **Being passionate for Jesus is the only passion that will not destroy us. All other passions will take over our lives.**

Inviting Jesus to be God of everything in our lives doesn't mean we will be perfect. But it does mean that—to the best of our knowledge—we submit everything in our lives to Him and seek Him as the source of our significance and security. How do we do that?

When we invite Jesus to be in charge of everything in our lives, He will show us areas that still need to be surrendered to Him— maybe even good and beautiful parts of our lives, but parts that in reality are not fully under His loving rule. We should not be shocked that we need to continually turn things over to His rule, even those things we thought we had given to Him. We are alive and growing, after all, not robots. Inviting Him to be God of everything in our lives means that we will keep learning through each episode in our journey. It means a life of learning and growing and discovering, continually keeping Him at the center—of everything.

When we invite Jesus to be God of everything in our lives, He becomes, in effect, the benevolent dictator of our hearts and the chief fascination of our imagination. He is the only one in the universe qualified to hold that place in our hearts. Because of His great love and goodness, He has earned the right to rule our lives so absolutely.

Pushing the Boundaries

Jesus will push the boundaries you—and others—have set in your life. He will help you see Him differently, and through that, help you live life differently. He is not about to put your will and mind into an involuntary state of altered reality. He will only challenge the boundaries you have set in your life if you are willing to rethink who He is and to reshape what it means to *follow*.

I have asked the Holy Spirit to show me aspects of living under His lordship, and I urge you to do the same. Why stop with one small insight, one tiny step in the journey? Only by giving everything to Jesus can we gain a fresh understanding of how to reset the boundaries in our lives. Allow Jesus, invite Him—indeed, dare to *want* Him—to be the strange, dangerous, unstoppable, unsettling, beautiful God-Man He is. Break out of your settled-routine understanding of life. Refuse to limit Him to the way you have known Him in the past. There is more to Jesus than you understand or see.

What Would Stop Jesus Being Lord of Your Life?

Imagine it this way: In your heart, there is a cross, and there is a throne. If you are seated on the throne of your life, then, in effect, Jesus is dead in you. You are on the throne, and Jesus is still hanging on the cross. You have

Allow Jesus, invite Him—indeed, dare to *want* Him—to be the strange, dangerous, unstoppable, unsettling, beautiful God-Man He is.

not invited Him to rule over you. If you come down off the throne and ask Jesus to take it and rule over you, you have made Jesus God of everything.

Far too many people following Jesus want all the advantages of a good and God-blessed life—prosperity, happiness, forgiveness, hope, and, yes, eternal life—but they do not want to pay the price of dying to their will and letting Jesus be God of everything.

What Does It Mean to Hand Over Control to Jesus?

Practically speaking, this means subjugating our will to His will and purposes. That means our plans, beliefs, dreams, and fears are placed under His control, no longer under our own. In that process, we continually learn to die to ourselves in the sense that we will not insist on living for what *we* want first but will be willing to put *His* purposes and *His* untamable desires above our own. The good news in this process of yielding to Jesus is that He is for us. He made us; He has good plans for us; and those plans fit into His awesome story.

God created Adam and Eve (and every human being since creation) for two great purposes: intimate friendship *with* God and purposeful living *for* God. In these two purposes for our lives we find ultimate fulfillment and happiness. Taking what God has given us and living independently of Him does not mean we are unable to enjoy life. But it does mean that we are missing the best God has for us, holding on to our understanding of pleasure and adventure and beauty instead of His, trusting our understanding more than His.

If we seek to bargain with God, then the love of God is cheapened and loses its grand meaning in our lives. There can be no compromise in inviting Jesus to be God of everything—friends, family, job, future plans, recreation, lifestyle, living situations, comfort zones; everything must be His and His alone. Jesus won't share His throne with any other god or idol, small or great, ugly or beautiful.

You might say, "But I'm doing pretty well. I live a good life. I'm a good person. I believe in God, and I have given my money and time to help people. I can only think of one or two small things I am holding back, but He is a God of love, after all—He won't mind." I don't want to shock you, but that is not enough. Jesus does not want control of 51 percent or even 98 percent of our lives. He wants to be in control of *all* areas—100 percent. Why would our loving Creator want less? Would He be God if He served our whims and demands? What kind of weak and diminished God would this be?

Picture your life like the chart below:

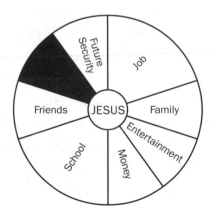

You might say, "I have given God everything except …" Is there one area that you still hold back from Him? If so, you are telling God which parts of your heart He can and can't rule. In effect, you are still ruling your life, treating God like your personal servant.

Even if you have given Him control over most of your life, you are really sitting on the throne of your heart and telling God which parts of your life are His. Do you really believe the Creator of the universe will accept this cozy arrangement? If you are trying to negotiate with God, you have not yet comprehended what it means to be a fully devoted follower of Jesus. You demean God's role as the loving but absolute leader in your life.

Going Two Ways at Once

Not only is it an insult to the Creator of the universe to give Him anything less than absolute control over our lives, but it is also a form of insanity. The most foolish thing a human can do is to refuse to give the all-wise, loving, absolutely pure, holy, just, forgiving, merciful Creator of the universe His rightful place over his or her life.

Imagine Bill at a soccer match. His friend Mark invites him out for a drink afterward. Since Bill would like to spend time with Mark, he accepts the invitation. A little while later, a second friend, Jerry, says to Bill, "I'd love to show you my new apartment." Bill would love to see his new apartment, so he agrees. After the match, Bill makes his way outside. Mark and Jerry are waiting. Their cars are parked side by side but headed in opposite directions. Since Bill wants to go with both of them, he puts one foot inside each car and says to both friends, "Let's go!" Both friends take off at once, and Bill finds himself in a very difficult situation!

Psychologists have a term for this: frustration. We can define this type of frustration as *having opposing goals*. People who attempt to live for themselves *and* for God are trying to go in two different directions spiritually at the same time; they will be *frustrated* people. There can be no peace in following Jesus if we are living this way.

Asking God to be first in our lives does not mean that we suddenly become religious extremists. Nor does it mean that we are perfect. What it does mean is that we submit everything to God; our understanding of surrendering to God will grow as He gives us more insight into His will for our lives. We go on a journey of learning and spiritual growth. At each new stage of the journey we face new challenges and decisions either to go our own way or to surrender to Him. This kind of relationship with Jesus will be dynamic and growing, not boring and confined. His loving rule is ever expanding and increasing and meaningful to us, so that we know more and more what it means to love Him fully and to be fully loved by Him.

The Motives behind Our Decisions

Loving Jesus by making Him Lord of everything in life also means discerning our motives for making those decisions and putting aside selfish motives in decision making. There are at least three basic levels of choices that every person makes:

Routine choices: These are the normal, everyday decisions made in business, family, and school, affecting everything from what clothes I wear, to what I eat, to what newspaper I read or music I listen to.

Major choices: These are the choices that have much greater implications for in life: Whom should I marry? What job should I take? Where should I live?

The ultimate choice: This choice can be made more than once, but it is made about only one thing—that is, whether or not I make Jesus the Lord of my life.

It is possible to make routine and major choices for God but on the ultimate level to continue to live selfishly. We could picture that in the following way:

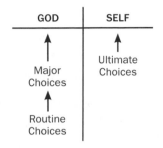

We can make decisions to attend church; give money to missions and the poor; or do other things "good Christians" do. However, if our ultimate motives are to impress other people or to gain a sense of importance, then our motives are selfish. And we fool ourselves if we think we are pleasing God. Doing all the right things for the wrong reasons means that all we have accomplished is a well-refined state of hypocrisy.

Peddling Pictures of Jesus

I'm a bit ashamed to say this, but in my high-school years I went door-to-door selling pictures of Jesus. Big prints, glossy and bright, two by three feet in size. I sold them for a margin of what they would have gone for in a decorating store or Christian bookshop. I bought them cheap from an uncle of mine, a professional door-to-door salesman, then peddled Jesus from house to house for a bargain.

I carried a nice selection of Jesuses; some that appealed to Catholics as well as those the Protestants preferred. I didn't think about why people would fork out hard-earned money for a big, unframed picture of Jesus, but looking back, I think I understand now. Hanging Jesus on the wall and having Him close by was a good deal. It didn't cost much, and He was there when you needed Him.

I carried enough prints of Jesus to fit everybody's preconceived ideas of what He was like. Do you need a meek and mild Jesus? Just happen to have Him. Jesus carrying a lamb? I have Him, too.

In the same way, we carry with us our mental pictures of Jesus. He is normally a cuddly, gentle, loving, and forgiving Jesus, there to help us in time of trouble. There are of course aspects of truth in those images of Jesus. But there is one huge problem with them: Far too often He is just too sweet and far too powerless.

I want you to reconsider Jesus. If necessary, trade in your mental pictures of Jesus for the real person. I'm not asking you to deny what Jesus has done for you in the past, but I am asking you not to limit Him. Consider the possibility that you have some wrong ideas about Him. No picture of Jesus on the wall of our home, and no mental picture of Jesus hanging on the walls of our heart, can fully represent Him. The danger with pictures is that we create them. They sometimes end up being images of ourselves that we project onto God.

Would You Reconsider Jesus?

Doing good things is often our way of trying to appease God, to buy Him off, to keep Him off our case. The result of doing good things for selfish reasons is religion. The Bible says this about religion, including "Christian" religion: "These things indeed have an appearance of wisdom in self-imposed religion, false humility, and neglect of the body, but are of no value against the indulgence of the flesh" (Col. 2:23 NKJV). *The Message* translates this verse so that it hits home in today's world: "Such things [religious things] sound impressive if said in a deep enough voice. They even give the illusion of being pious and humble and ascetic. But they're just another way of showing off, making yourselves look important."

In other words, it is possible for us to call ourselves Christians, to do good things for Jesus, and ultimately to die without ever surrendering everything in life to God. Jesus said, "Knowing the correct password—saying 'Master, Master,' for instance—isn't going to get you anywhere with me. What is required is serious obedience—*doing* what my Father wills" (Matt. 7:21 MSG).

Doing the will of God is not just about *what* we do but *why* we do it. Jesus hated the hypocrisy of the religious show-offs of His day because they had turned loving God into a religious performance. They used it to control and manipulate other people's lives. It is so important that we make Jesus our Lord from a motive to please Him, and not to get something from Him.

Our motivation for making Jesus the Lord of our lives should not be to get into heaven, to impress God with our spirituality, or to try to get God to love us. Nor should it be to impress others. Jesus wants us to choose Him to be the God of everything

Doing good things for God without loving Jesus is turning our Christian faith into one more religion— exactly what the world does not need.

for one reason only: because we have fallen deeply in love with Him. Loving God is not about duty to God but delight in God. Doing good things for God without loving Jesus is turning our Christian faith into one more religion—exactly what the world does not need.

Are You Holding Back on God?

As you have read through this chapter, it may have become apparent to you that you have held things back from God or are serving Him with wrong motives. Do you have Jesus framed and hanging on the wall of your heart, a nice adornment, but not the wild ruler of your life? Then you desperately need to repent and return to God. Remember the story of the lost son (Luke 15:11–32)? The older brother needed to return to the father as badly as the lost son did.

Are there aspects of your life that you have held back from Him? Are there dimensions of your life that you have not put under His rule? Perhaps you have even come to the startling discovery—which some professing Christians do—that all your life you have been doing good deeds, but your motivation has been selfish.

If you have made that kind of discovery, there is only one adequate response. I encourage you to bow before the Lord Jesus, confess your desperate need of Him, ask Him to forgive you for your selfishness, and choose to make Him the Lord of *everything* in your life. Receive by faith the forgiveness of your sins (1 John 1:6–9).

Take time to think through what this means. Read and think deeply about who Jesus is as Lord of everything. When you do make the choice, please do so knowing that the Lord Jesus loves you deeply … but also remember that He refuses to take second or third place in your life. His plan for your life is good, and His world needs your total-surrender involvement. His desire to rule over your life is motivated by His love for you and His commitment to share a relationship with you that liberates you to be all He created you to be. When we put Jesus first in our lives, we unleash the power of the Creator of the universe to dwell within us and to work through us. The resurrected, infinite, all-powerful Creator comes to live inside us and empower us to serve others. This act of surrendering to God is your way of saying you want to love God and you want Him to be God of everything in your life, good and bad, beautiful and ugly. All of you. Everything about you. For all of Him and all He purposes to do through you for others.

It is no small thing to invite Jesus to be your Savior and Lord. You and I, as creatures, are acknowledging we are made by the Creator. As we read in God's Story, Great One wants to be our friend. We see now more fully than ever before that we have been in rebellion against Him but that we want to return to Him. When this happens, not only do we commit ourselves to Him, but we allow Him to be committed to us and committed to do His will through us for others. In making that commitment, Jesus says, "I will guarantee your ultimate victory. As long as you will submit to Me, I will ensure your victory over sin and I will live through you for the sake of others."

Making Jesus the Lord of everything can be a painful process, because it means giving to Jesus the big and little "idols" of our lives. These idols can work their way into our identity and our sense of significance until we are no longer our true selves. We become what we imagine we are, rather than the people God made us to be. Tearing down something that has taken a place of idolatrous devotion in our hearts is like tearing out a piece of our own flesh.

The Bible calls this painful and radical recalibrating of our lives *repentance*. The act of repenting is terrifying and at the same time liberating. It is not a step everyone is willing to take, but when we do, we are transformed.

Reflecting and Responding

1. Do a discovery Bible study on Luke 9:57–62. (See the end of chapter 2 for a fuller explanation.)

2. How do you feel when you read these words: "Jesus does not want 51 percent or even 98 percent control of our lives"? How do these words apply to your life?

3. What mental pictures of Jesus do you have that could be a substitute for the real Jesus?

4. Why are our motives so important in the decision to give God control of everything in our lives?

5. Making Jesus ruler of everything in our lives means rethinking what we understand about God, church, mission, etc., in the light of who Jesus is. What changes have started taking place for you as you rethink what you believe and practice?

FOUR

Repentance

Repentance is the connecting point between our old way of life and the new; between following Jesus on our terms and following Him on His. Repentance is a change of mind about the direction we are going, how we have been living, and what we have believed about God and the world. It is a total turnaround in our thinking and living. Repentance is not merely a feeling of remorse that unexpectedly sweeps over us. And it is much more than wishing we hadn't done something that has backfired on us.

The question, then, is, when do we know we have truly repented of something? How do we know we are truly serious about following Jesus?

We are told in 2 Corinthians 7:10 that there is a difference between godly sorrow and worldly sorrow for sin. Godly sorrow is *repentance;* worldly sorrow is *regret.* Repentance implies that, if we had the opportunity to commit that sin again, we would not. But regret suggests that we would do it again in such a way as to try to avoid the consequences or make sure we weren't caught.

Consider an unmarried couple who are sexually involved. If the woman gets pregnant, they may either regret not taking proper precautions, or they may repent of having had sex outside of marriage because they know it is wrong. Repentance means they see the intrinsic wrong of their sin. Regret means they are simply sorry for the consequences.

Brokenhearted God

In God's Story, He is the offended party. He is the one that has been wronged, not us. True repentance occurs when we begin to see sin from God's point of view—when we see the way our sin has broken His heart. In Genesis 6:5–6 we are told, "Then the LORD saw that the wickedness of man was great on the earth, and that every intent of the thoughts of his heart was only evil continually. The LORD was sorry that He had made man on the earth, and He was grieved in His heart" (NASB). God was so disappointed with what He saw that there was a great sorrow in His heart—to the point that He regretted creating us. What we do affects God deeply.

Jesus also was brokenhearted. It says in one verse that He wept over Jerusalem because of her sins: "O Jerusalem, Jerusalem, the one who kills the prophets and stones those who are sent to her! How often I wanted to gather your children together, as a hen gathers her brood under her wings, but you were not willing!" (Luke 13:34 NKJV). His heart ached over the religious pride of the Jews, not because their sins were on His list of dos and don'ts, but because sin is contrary to His very nature.

True repentance occurs when we begin to see sin from God's point of view— when we see the way our sin has broken His heart.

If we want to love Jesus as His followers, then we must see sin and self-centeredness from His perspective. No ranting sermon on hell can ever change a person's heart. But seeing the grief sin has brought to the heart of the One who created us can get through to us … if we allow ourselves to feel what God feels toward sin—our sin.

That will only happen when we ask God to show us what our sin does to Him. Then we will begin to understand His great love for us despite how much we have hurt Him and grieved His heart. Turning away from that sin becomes the natural thing to do. This is the test of our sincerity and of the level of our desperation to be right with God.

When I use the word *sin,* I'm thinking of everything from speaking rudely or crudely to people, to racism and economic injustice. Sin can be personal and it can be systemic in a culture or nation.

The great nineteenth-century American evangelist Charles Finney refused people who begged him to pray with them a "sinner's prayer." He told them they needed more time to consider the seriousness of their choice. This may seem hard, but, as a result, Finney had a very high rate of converts who lived for Christ all their lives because he did all that was possible to ensure their full repentance. I wonder sometimes if much of the "backsliding" we hear of today happens because we have eased people into conversion without repentance.

Finney wanted people to count the cost. He wanted to know if they were serious enough to pay the price of repentance. *Repentance* literally means to change one's mind. To repent is to turn from loving ourselves supremely to loving God first.

The Holy Spirit's Work in Our Hearts!

The Holy Spirit is continually at work in our hearts to help us respond with godly sorrow toward sin. Repentance is not a one-time thing, something we do when we choose to follow Jesus. Repentance is a lifestyle. It is deciding that we are going to deal honestly with things as they come up in our lives. It doesn't mean we plan to sin, but it does mean that, knowing that we will sin at times, we choose to deal with sin by confessing it to God and to those impacted by our sin.

When I use the word *sin,* I'm thinking of everything from speaking rudely or crudely to people, to racism and economic injustice. Sin can be personal and it can be systemic in a culture or nation. Sin covers a broad range of actions and thoughts, from failing to keep a promise in a business deal, to human trafficking. Although private sin and national sin by no means have the same impact on people's lives, both warrant the same response—repentance.

Paul asks in Romans 2:4, "Do you presume on the riches of his kindness and forbearance and patience, not knowing that God's kindness is meant to lead you to repentance?" (ESV). By continually reminding ourselves of God's rich kindness, forbearance, and patience, we are motivated to repent continually of sin when we see it in our lives.

Circles of Confession

The "circles of confession" describe the extent our sins have impacted other people. Some sins are secretly committed in our hearts, others are personal against another individual, and still others are "public" in nature. Think of the circles of confession as concentric circles, with private sins in the inner circle, personal sins in the next circle, and public sins that impact groups of people in the outer circle. The

Bible teaches that followers of Jesus are to confess every sin to God, and sins against individuals and groups of people are to be confessed to those we sin against as well as to God.

CIRCLES OF CONFESSION

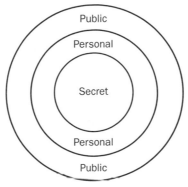

If a person's sin is a private sin of the heart (for example, if you have had impure or critical thoughts toward another person and he or she is unaware of it) then it is a matter between you and God alone. To go to that person and confess your sin in this instance can cause unnecessary damage to the person and to your relationship with him or her. But if it is a personal sin that involved another person, then your sin is against both God and that individual and should be confessed to both God and that person. If you sinned against a group of people and the consequences of your sin have affected their lives, you owe both God and those people your confession and repentance.

Many years ago, I came to a crisis point in my relationship with others. Through impatience and unkindness, I had hurt several close friends deeply, shown disrespect for my wife, and was struggling in my relationship with God. I went for a walk one day to be alone. I decided to put my life totally on the line for the Lord. I knew at that

point that it had to be all or nothing. No superficial response could
deal with the crisis I had created for myself.

I confessed my predicament to the Lord, acknowledged my sin,
and then prayed: "Lord, I desperately need You right now. I choose
not to go around this situation. I ask you to use this time in my life
to bring me to a place of brokenness. Do anything You need to do in
my life to produce humility and Christlikeness in me.

"I ask You to be ruthless in dealing with my sin. No matter how
long it takes, Lord, or what You have to do, I welcome Your loving
judgment in my heart. Expose anything and everything in my life
You want to deal with. No matter what the cost, Lord, I commit
myself to doing things Your way. I refuse to hide my sin or to avoid
Your dealing with my character. I don't want any shortcuts to my
growth. Even if it takes years, I say yes to You, Lord."

At that point in my life, God began a deeper work of repentance
in my character. I invited His refining fire, no matter how hot it
got—and it did get very hot. I asked for His bright light of truth to
be turned upon my heart, no matter what was there and no matter
who found out. I asked God to produce spiritual brokenness in me,
no matter how long it took. I committed myself to be ruthless with
my sin. I decided to take the attitude that in every conflict I had with
others from then on, I would believe that God wanted to use the
conflict to show me what He wanted to change in my heart and life.

As L. E. Maxwell says,

> Many people wonder why they have no victory over
> their wounded pride, their touchiness, their greedi-
> ness … the secret is not far away. They secretly

and habitually practice shrine worship—at the shrine of self. In the outward Cross they glory, but inwardly they worship another god and stretch out their hands to serve a pitied, petty and pampered self-life. Until Christ works out in you an inner crucifixion which will cut you off from self-infatuation and unite you to God in a deep union of love, a thousand heavens could not give you peace.[1]

I ask you today, right now, to make that same commitment I made years ago, and still hold to with all my heart. I cannot express to you how glad I am that I have chosen God's way. God has been faithful to me, and I rejoice that He has answered my prayer.

Reflecting and Responding

1. Do a discovery Bible study on 2 Corinthians 7:10–11.

2. Have you experienced the difference between worldly and godly sorrow? Describe what happened and how you learned the difference.

3. Take time to pray about the differences in the circles of confession and how you would apply them to your life now. Is there someone you need to go to in order to make things right?

4. Who is the most offended party when we sin? How does one develop an awareness of how sin brings sorrow to the heart of God?

FIVE

Pride

There are seven deadly sins that God hates, and pride heads the list:

> *These six things the LORD hates, yes, seven are an abomination to Him: a proud look, a lying tongue, hands that shed innocent blood, a heart that devises wicked plans, feet that are swift in running to evil, a false witness who speaks lies, and one who sows discord among brethren. (Prov. 6:16–19 NKJV)*

The Root of Pride

Pride grows deep within us, unseen, like the roots of an unwanted weed in the garden. It flourishes deep inside our hearts, in the dark places hidden from others and sometimes even from ourselves.

Pride is an undue sense of self-importance. It is pretending to be something we are not, refusing to acknowledge our weaknesses or recognize our natural limitations. Pride is covering our problems or sins from those with whom we should be open and hiding behind excuses and rationalizations when confronted. Pride will eventually deceive us and blind us to its working in our lives (Obad. 1:3). In a word, pride is the unseen sin, the cancer of the heart.

Some confusion may occur when we talk of pride. We can talk about being proud of our achievements and abilities, proud of our spouses and proud of our children, but none of these is what the Bible calls *pride*.

Pride, as defined in the Bible, is choosing our own way. It says to God, "I'll do this my way. Don't interfere in my life. When I need you, I'll call." In the context of God's Story, pride is the root of rebellion. Consciously or unconsciously, pride works in us to lead us to rebellion against God.

The greatest hindrance to knowing God and experiencing loving relationships is pride. The greatest obstacle to loving other people is our pride. The greatest barrier to serving the poor and sharing our love for Jesus with those who don't know Him is pride. Every sin committed can be traced back to pride; every war, every instance of human conflict, every divided family, can be traced back to pride.

The greatest obstacle to loving other people is our pride.

This is not just my opinion, but what the Bible teaches. Listen to these words from James 4:1: "Where do you think all these appalling wars and quarrels come from? Do you think they just happen? Think again. They come about because you want your own way, and fight for it deep inside yourselves. You lust for what you don't have and are willing to kill to get it. You want what isn't yours and will risk violence to get your hands on it" (MSG).

The Bible speaks in very strong terms about God's attitude toward pride. In Proverbs we read: "The LORD detests all the proud of heart.... Pride goes before destruction" (Prov. 16:5, 18).

Pride is very subtle. You don't wake up in the morning and say to yourself, "At three o'clock today I am going to indulge in a pride attack." Pride does not come upon you in a sudden, violent way. It is treacherous. C. S. Lewis described the problem of pride perfectly:

> There is no fault which we are more unconscious of in ourselves; and the more we have it in ourselves, the more we dislike it in others.... It is pride that has been the chief cause of misery in every nation and family since the world began.... It is enmity not only between man and man, but between man and God. In God you come up against something that is in every respect immeasurably superior to yourself. Unless you know God as that and there-fore know yourself as nothing in comparison, you do not know God at all. As long as you are proud, you cannot know God.[1]

I have found it very difficult to discern pride in my own life. It is deceptive. I have desperately needed God and others to help me see the pride in my life. I am convinced that God will reveal the pride in our hearts if we ask Him.

The Root Grows Where the Soil Is Favorable

Pride will grow wherever the conditions of one's heart are favorable. Paul wrote to one church to remind them of the dangers of pride. "Let us not become conceited, provoking one another, envying one another...." (Gal. 5:26 NKJV).

Jesus also had to deal with pride in His disciples. James and John thought they had things worked out quite well for themselves. In heaven, one would sit on Jesus' right side, the other on His left. All they wanted was for Jesus to use His "influence" in arranging things with the Father (Mark 10:35–41). However, instead of His cooperation they received a lesson in humility with this rebuke: "'You've observed how godless rulers throw their weight around,' He said, 'and when people get a little power how quickly it goes to their heads'" (Mark 10:42–43 MSG).

Throughout church history, pride has wrought havoc, creating bitterness, division, and strife, and we should not assume that we are any less susceptible. The root goes deep in every human heart. To detect pride in our lives we need to look for its outward manifestations—the fruit that reveals the root.

The Author of Pride

The Bible is very explicit about who the author of pride is—Satan himself. If we take Isaiah 14 as an allegorical narrative, Satan is recorded as saying this about himself:

> *You said to yourself, "I'll climb to heaven. I'll set my throne over the stars of God. I'll run the assembly of angels that meets on sacred Mount Zaphon. I'll climb*

> *to the top of the clouds. I'll take over as King of the*
> *Universe!" (Isa. 14:13–14 MSG).*

Satan's emphasis was on the things he thought he could do, but the last claim is perhaps the most revealing—he believed he had the ability to make himself like God, to take over as king of the universe. Notice how many times the word *I* occurs in the passage. Satan scorned dependence on God, choosing instead to rely on his own wisdom and way of doing things.

Down through the centuries, these same thoughts have been expressed again and again. All of us have allowed and encouraged pride to grow in our hearts. We continue to believe we can do things without God. We think we can take God's place and steer our lives in any direction we choose. We try to make God a sort of good-luck charm to be called upon in times of personal emergency.

The bottom line is this: If we love Jesus and welcome Him to be God of absolutely everything in our lives, if we are to put Him and His purposes for our lives first, we must take a radical step of humility. Are you ready to take that step?

The character of God and pride form opposite ends of a scale. God is the author and perfecter of humility; Satan is the author and perfecter of pride. The two cannot coexist. We must decide to whom we will give our allegiance and seek to imitate in our attitudes and choices.

Pride and Our Relationship to God

We are God's creation. He intricately designed and brought each of us into being. He knows all there is to know about us.

In every way, God is vastly superior to His creation. He is infinite; we are finite. He is righteous; we are unrighteous. He is wise; we are foolish. He is ever the same; we are changeable. Those who refuse to honor God, who deny Him or underestimate His power, err to the point of ludicrousness. Pride is a form of moral insanity. If we fail to see God as immeasurably superior to ourselves, we fail to see Him at all. In confining God to our limited concepts of who He is, we in essence deny Him His loving right to be the ruler of our lives.

In order to love God, we need to respond to His love humbly. We must acknowledge His vastly superior wisdom, strength, and knowledge. Pride will hinder our ability to do this. If we fail to do it, we will eventually be cut off from God. This may seem harsh. "Surely," we reason, "a little pride will not hurt. After all, nobody is perfect."

The Bible, however, allows no such concession to this deadly sin. God is merciful, but the Bible speaks unequivocally about God's reaction to pride. Pride is an abomination to Him (Prov. 16:5, 18), and He will not tolerate it. Pride will not only hurt our relationships with God; the Bible says God goes out of His way to oppose and resist the proud person (James 4:6).

Faced with this, we have two choices. Either we cooperate with God and ask for His help in dealing with pride in our lives, or we face alienation and separation from our Maker. As we move on and look more closely at the root of pride and the destruction it brings, we will begin to understand why pride is such an abomination to God.

Pride and Our Relationship to Others

Pride alienates us from people. If we judge others, if we deem them as either inferior or superior to us, it will affect all our relationships.

If we think people are inferior, then we feel justified in putting them down or simply ignoring them. If, on the other hand, we think them superior, we feel put down and unworthy. In this situation, our pride turns on us, enslaving us in a preoccupation with what others think.

We all sin. Sadly, sometimes another's sin may hurt us or wound us deeply—we may even want to hurt that person back. And we are faced with a choice: We can either repent of our resentment, forgive the person for what he or she has done to us, and set the matter right, or we can continue on the path we have set for ourselves—a path that leads straight to destruction. Forgiving a person who has hurt us frees us from the bondage of bitterness and allows us to grow emotionally and spiritually. Forgiving a person who is abusive does not mean that we need to submit ourselves to him or her, but that through forgiveness we are freed to move forward in life. Pride clouds our ability to see a situation as God sees it, while humility enables us to discern the sin of others and, at the same time, to forgive them.

Pride cripples our ability to get along with others and leaves us isolated and alone. It sets husband against wife, parent against child, friend against friend, and race against race. It leaves us with our hurt, which—if left unchecked—will harden into hatred and alienation.

Proud Christians also divide church communities. Pride, not doctrine, divides individual Christians and entire congregations from one another as people murmur against their leaders, judge their fellow believers, and secretly promote division, all in the name of being concerned for what is true. They alienate themselves and their fellow believers as well as those who look to Christians to be an example.

Pride and Ourselves

Not only does pride destroy our relationships with God and others, but it also wreaks havoc in our own lives. Proverbs 26:12 tells us there is one thing worse than a fool, and that is a proud man. Indeed, a proud man is the biggest fool of all because his pride will bring him low, leading to his personal destruction (Prov. 29:23).

A teachable spirit and a willingness to learn from others is the greatest protection from the consequences of other people's sins against us. As strange as it may seem, the greatest release from hurt, rejection, and emotional damage from other people is humility. It protects us from problems that we otherwise have no control over.

Many times in my life, I have had to rely on others for help in recognizing my own pride. If you ask God to reveal pride to you, don't be surprised if others point out weaknesses in your life. When confronted, it is not always easy to admit we are wrong. But if we are to enjoy the blessing of humility, admitting wrong is imperative.

My wife, Sally, and I sometimes disagree about important decisions. When disagreements arise, we sometimes take sides and argue. I tend to harden my attitude, and before long, I can drag other issues into the disagreement. After one such encounter, when Sally told me she felt I was becoming judgmental and harsh, I came to see that my focus was no longer on what was best for our family but on getting my own way. It was hard to admit at first, but she was right. When this happens, my objective has shifted from making the best decision to trying to prove I am right.

God's intention in revealing pride in our lives is always for our benefit. He wants to help us, not humiliate us. Generation after generation, God, with great sadness, has seen the destruction wrought by pride in the lives of His children. He longs for us to be freed by taking the crucial step of humbling ourselves before Him and others.

How to See the Unseeable Sin of Pride

The symptoms of pride can be likened to those of cancer. At first, we're unaware of it, and it grows unnoticed. Slowly, we become aware that something is not functioning as it should. A leg aches, we feel nauseated, or a lump begins to grow in our body. Now we are faced with two choices: either go to a doctor for diagnosis and treatment or pretend nothing is wrong. In the early stages it is easy to hide the symptoms from others, but as time goes by it becomes more difficult. We can no longer walk without an exaggerated limp, or face eating a meal, or even talk because of the pain in our body. The once insignificant growth has become a consuming and potentially fatal illness.

So it is with pride. At first, the symptoms are almost unnoticeable—we become a little impatient when inconvenienced; we avoid certain people; it takes a little longer to forgive someone; we struggle to say "You're right, I'm wrong" when corrected. Again, we have two choices: either ignore these symptoms as insignificant or go to God and ask Him to show us the root of the problem and help us deal with it. If we ignore the fruit of pride, the root will continue to grow and spread until everyone can see the cancer consuming us.

Jesus once said of people who are hypocritical and full of pride, "You can detect them by the way they act, just as you can identify a tree by its fruit. You don't pick grapes from thorn bushes, or figs from thistles" (Matt. 7:16 NLT). Jesus was saying we can detect the root of pride by its fruit in our lives.

Jesus taught His disciples that those watching their lives would know they were His followers by how they loved and cared for one another. Fully devoted followers of Jesus take His command to love one another seriously. Those who are watching the present-day disciples of Jesus will notice how real we are and whether we take time for one another. We know this cannot happen by merely attending church meetings for an hour or two on a Sunday. And when we do spend time with one another, we have to face the reality that we may not actually like every member of the community we are part of.

Transparency

Transparency is a willingness to be known for who we really are, to be ruthlessly honest about our lives. Either we will take steps to be transparent, or we will hide our secrets. There is no in-between place with God. You are either in the light or hiding in the dark.

The greatest hindrance to transparency is our pride. It gets in the way of opening our lives to other people. We can either retreat from the ones we don't like, taking the easy way of avoidance, pretending we like them with a sweet but insincere smile; or we can decide to grow beyond our reactions and learn to love people when it is hard to do so. We all need to commit ourselves to be open to one another and to receive correction from one another, where necessary.

Let's look more closely at the fruit of pride; or, to put it another way, the fruit that reveals the root, which is pride. (I'm not "proud" of the list—it came from personal failures and God's dealings in my life. But I pass it on, knowing that humility truly does liberate us from pride.) Each of the following sections begins with a passage of Scripture followed by a description. Don't rush past this next section.

You may want to meditate and pray through it, one section at a time, possibly even one a day. I suggest going through it on your own, asking God to do a deep, radical, and life-changing work in your heart. And I suggest going through it with other believers in your community, acknowledging your faults and weaknesses and praying for one another as you do.

The Root and the Fruit of Pride

Stealing from God

> I am the LORD; that is my name! I will not give my glory to anyone else. I will not share my praise with carved idols. (Isa. 42:8 NLT)

Each of us has gifts and abilities that God has placed within us, things like a beautiful singing voice, organizational abilities, or gardening skills. Some are gifted with keen minds and prophetic insight. An honest estimation of our gifts is necessary if we are to develop the talents God has invested in us. However, a dangerous form of pride can cause us to take credit for the gifts God has given us. By giving the impression that we are in some way solely responsible for these gifts, we take the glory away from God, and God has warned, "I will not yield my glory to another" (Isa. 48:11). Taking credit for the good that God has enabled us to do is stealing from God.

Taking credit for the good that God has enabled us to do is stealing from God.

Callousness to the plight of the poor

Listen to me, dear brothers and sisters. Hasn't God chosen the poor in this world to be rich in faith? Aren't they the ones who will inherit the Kingdom he promised to those who love him? And yet, you insult the poor man! (James 2:5–6 NLT)

Pride makes us feel like we deserve what we have, and the poor have what they deserve as well. A proud person never stops to consider that he or she has done nothing to deserve being born with wealth or security. Have you bothered to reflect on how you would react if you were born in a one-room shack, in destitute poverty?

Self-centeredness

God has given gifts to each of you from his great variety of spiritual gifts. Manage them well so that God's generosity can flow through you. (1 Peter 4:10 NLT)

There are those of us who use a facade of "spirituality" to cover inward selfishness. If, in using our gifts and abilities, we are simply seeking our own benefit and making ourselves appear good to others, we are self-centered. Self-centered pride feeds a desire to be served, to be right, to be noticed. It says: "Do it my way; this is my ministry, my vision, my plan." The underlying assumption is, "I deserve this."

Notice how shallow this attitude is compared to Paul's response to the Corinthians: "It is God who gives us spiritual gifts. If we use them generously, then God will work through us for the benefit of others" (2 Cor. 12:15, author's paraphrase).

In this light, I have good news for you: God does not want to hurt your pride—He wants to kill it! Only through a deathblow at the heart of our egotism and self-centeredness can we become the people God created us to be.

> **I have good news for you: God does not want to hurt your pride—He wants to kill it!**

A demanding attitude

> *I know what it is to be in need, and I know what it is to have plenty. I have learned the secret of being content in any and every situation, whether well fed or hungry, whether living in plenty or in want. (Phil. 4:12, author's paraphrase)*

Demanding people reveal their pride by constantly bringing attention to things that have not been done for them. By demanding that others do things their way, they are in essence saying, "I am superior to you. I deserve to have it my way." They look out for their rights; they feel entitled to what they think they deserve, seemingly oblivious to the fact that what all of us "deserve" is eternal separation from God.

Those who recognize that this form of pride inhabits their hearts, and have cried out in repentance and asked for forgiveness from it, experience a deep sense of gratitude when they receive forgiveness. They realize that everything outside of hell is grace.

Superiority

*Live in harmony with each other. Don't try to act
important, but enjoy the company of ordinary people.
And don't think you know it all! (Rom. 12:16 NLT)*

Pride causes us to feel that we are more important than others.
Those who believe they are superior to others, whether consciously or
unconsciously, have an inner attitude of condescension, a belief that
somehow they are closer to God or just better than other people. It is
pride—not doctrines or disagreements or political differences or race or
poverty—that causes so much of our division. If only we truly believed
in our hearts that we need others who are different from us, then dis-
unity, church divisions, mistrust, and racial conflict would evaporate.

Do you look down on people who have not had your spiritual
experience; who are from another racial group, denomination, age
group; or who are members of the opposite sex? Are there Christians
you are uncomfortable having fellowship with simply because of
their beliefs or spiritual gifts? By refusing to associate with some
people and passively avoiding other groups of people, we expose the
pride in our hearts.

I once commented to a friend that I would not associate with
a certain group of Christians because of their aberrant theology. In
my eyes, they were doing more harm than good. I conceded that
they were indeed Christians, but I felt they should be avoided at all
costs. My friend challenged this attitude. She did not defend their
beliefs, but she pointed out that my attitudes and actions were not
like Jesus and, in fact, were rooted in pride. As I prayed about my

friend's exhortations, I began to see that the greater problem was not the poor theology of those I disagreed with but my own arrogance. I was dissociating myself from those Christ gave His name to, those He died for and adopted as His own children (Eph. 2:14).

Sarcasm

> *No man can tame the tongue. It is a restless evil, full of deadly poison.... But if you harbor bitter envy and selfish ambition in your hearts, do not boast about it or deny the truth. (James 3:8, 14)*

Caustic comments may be socially acceptable, but they have no place among followers of Jesus. Sarcasm is a thinly veiled attempt to impress people by highlighting the faults of others. Sarcasm is fueled by humor at the expense of other people.

Jesus never used sarcasm when dealing with His disciples. When a problem arose, He spoke directly to the people involved, not behind their backs. Let us take His example and deal straightforwardly with issues between us instead of resorting to sarcasm. And let us repent of all humor that makes people of other races or nationalities the brunt of our jokes. What is funny to you may grieve God.

A critical attitude

> *Don't use cruel or abusive language. Let everything you say be motivated by grace and kindness, so that your words will be an encouragement to those who hear them.*

*Take a lifelong break from all cutting, backbiting, and
demeaning talk. (Eph. 4:29, 32, author's paraphrase)*

Proud people are critical and judgmental. They have difficulty
seeing the good in others and are quick to negate the positive through
a critical word. In judging another person we are actually saying, "I
can do better. Why don't you just move over and let me do it?"

When we speak against a fellow Christian, we speak against
and grieve the Holy Spirit. Slander, gossip, and negative speech are
divisive and destructive. Speak about others the way you would like
them to speak about you.

Do you speak casually about the faults of others? Do you derive
a secret enjoyment from hearing bad news about other people? Think
about how destructive words can be. I would say that you don't have
to lie to slander someone. Just speaking the truth about people's
weaknesses can undermine them.

Impatience

*Love is very patient, love is always kind, and is not
jealous or boastful; love does not brag and is not
arrogant, love is not rude and irritable. Love is not
demanding. Love keeps no record of when it has been
wronged, and does not wrong others in return. (1 Cor.
13:4–5, author's paraphrase)*

By being impatient, we signify that our ideas, projects, programs, and schedules are more important than those of other people.

When we fail, we justify our lack of love and self-control and express it through reacting or lashing out. We often have to wait for others, but becoming impatient at such times, regardless of whether it is the other person's fault, is never justified. I have found I am most impatient when I think I'm right. I want to forge ahead with implementing my ideas and therefore sometimes fail to see the value of listening to the suggestions of others.

Envy and greed

> *Watch out! Beware of covetousness, for one's life does*
> *not consist in the abundance of the things he possesses.*
> *(Luke 12:15, author's paraphrase)*

Envy and greed stem from a belief that we have a right to more than we currently have. Jesus explicitly tells us not to put our trust in material things. If He had to warn people of His day to beware of being overcome by greed and covetousness, how much more should we be on guard in our materialistic world? Greed fills our hearts with longing for more—more money and more possessions. Instead of focusing on being content with what we have, we constantly seek those things we do not have.

Greed is a way of looking at the world, a way that has little to do with what we actually have. I have seen beggars on the streets of Mumbai who were more generous with the little they had than some well-off Christians. Lack of generosity infects our spirit and robs us of our hunger for spiritual reality. Greed dulls the spiritual side of a person.

Lack of forgiveness

Bless your enemies; no cursing under your breath.
Laugh with your happy friends when they're happy;
share tears when they're down. (Rom. 12:14–15 MSG)

If, after being persecuted or rejected by someone, we do not make a conscious effort to forgive, we are in danger of becoming hard-hearted. In that state, it is easy to rationalize bitterness and hostility by focusing on the injustice done to us. At first, we focus only on the person who has hurt us, but once we have started down this path, we discover that it cannot be applied selectively. One's whole life can soon be consumed by bitterness. The only cure is forgiveness.

Forgiveness is a powerful force. Through God's forgiveness of us, and our subsequent forgiveness of others, we experience true love for God and for one another. Through forgiving those who sin against us, we find new freedom in our hearts.

An unteachable attitude

They did not obey or incline their ear, but walked in their
own counsels and in the stubbornness of their evil heart,
and went backward and not forward. (Jer. 7:24 NASB)

None of us is above the need for correction in some area of life. When confronted by someone, do you listen, or do you ignore what that person has to say? Do you accept reproof or become resentful that someone would dare correct you? Do you rationalize, excuse, or explain? Do you come out on the defensive?

The more mature we become, the more we welcome the input and correction of others—from our enemies and those with opposing views as well as from friends and those we agree with. In laying aside our pride, we benefit from the insights of many wise and godly people, and sometimes also from the ungodly.

But being teachable is not just about receiving correction. A teachable person is one who seeks advice, welcomes the counsel of others, and is a lifetime learner. Teachable people ask questions, listen to what others say, and are constantly learning. Teachable people have an open attitude to people of other political and religious persuasions. The Bible describes this sort of person in James 3:15–17. One translation of these verses says a wise person is "open to reason" (RSV). Another says they are "willing to yield" (NKJV).

People-pleasing

> *Then Saul finally admitted, "Yes, I have sinned. I have disobeyed your instructions and the Lord's command, for I was afraid of the people and did what they demanded" (1 Sam. 15:24 NLT).*

We can easily become slaves to other people's opinions and not live to please God. Jesus told a man who wanted to bury his father before making a commitment, "Let the dead bury their own dead" (Luke 9:60). Jesus identified the idol in this man's heart and asked him to put Him first, above his family. In the Beatitudes Jesus says,

"Blessed are you when men hate you, when they exclude you and insult you and reject your name as evil, because of the Son of Man. Rejoice in that day and leap for joy" (Luke 6:22–23).

There are times when we must follow God, even if that means not pleasing others. The more ungodly the people around us are, the more likely we will have to make a decision that they will consider offensive. Of course, if you are to be persecuted, make sure it is because of obeying Jesus and not because of your own foolishness or pride.

By trying to please people and live up to their expectations, we can easily fall into a false form of spirituality. We find ourselves praying, reading Scripture, and worshipping not from the heart but from a secret motive to impress others. We become more interested in how we look to others than how we look to God. The more insecure we are, the more susceptible we become to the opinions of others. Humility frees us from this form of pride, allowing us to live to please the Lord.

Flattery

A flattering mouth works ruin. (Prov. 26:28 NKJV)

Compliments and flattery are not the same thing. When someone offers a sincere compliment, his or her aim is to encourage and uplift the other person. The person who is a flatterer, however, has a different motive. Flattery is often used as bait, dangled before people to probe their loyalties and vulnerabilities. If the bait is taken, the flatterer has found a weakness to be exploited. Flattery is designed to manipulate—to win another person's favor by saying things about that person pleasing to him or her.

Look at the way flattery is worded, and you will clearly see this: "You're so much more understanding than my husband." "I can trust you." "You're not like other Christians I've met. I can tell you really love me." On the surface, these seem to be compliments, but in them is a competitive edge, a temptation to compare with others deemed inferior, and a subtle appeal to pride. The motive behind the words is insincere.

What can be done about flattery? If we are in the habit of flattering others, then we must stop. It is a form of manipulation and selfishness. Ask God to show you the root of pride behind your sin.

Self-pity

> Be joyful always; pray continually; give thanks in all
> circumstances, for this is God's will for you in Christ
> Jesus. (1 Thess. 5:16–18)

Self-pity is a direct result of failing to turn our problems over to the Lord. By clinging to our hurts, frustrations, and disappointments, we blame God and others, and I believe that some of us use pity in order to get attention or to get our own way.

One day I lapsed into a bout of self-pity. I was feeling sorry for myself, thinking there was no hope in my situation: "Nobody understands me. Nobody cares about my needs, yet I always have to look out for their needs. I don't want this responsibility anymore." In that frame of mind, I caught a ferry across the harbor in Amsterdam, where we were living at the time, and sat alone on the far bank. I poured my heart out to God. "I don't think I can keep doing this. I can't handle the pressure." It was one great pity party.

In His kindness, the Lord answered me—but not in the way I had expected. He told me He wanted to *expand* me. He wanted me to do more, and if I allowed Him free rein in my life, He would increase my capacity for the job and my love for the people I was working with. Something broke inside me that day. It was my pride. I had been trying to carry things on my own and had not been asking the Lord for His help. I wanted people to know what a hero I was and to feel sorry for me. I had failed to see that the burdens and responsibilities I was carrying were not mine to carry alone, and as a result, I had fallen into self-pity.

When we are hurt, used, presumed upon, misunderstood, oppressed, or sinned against, it is easy to lapse into self-pity. There is a place for resisting abuse and mistreatment. But it is very easy to allow *thought patterns* of self-pity to establish themselves if we are disappointed in people. Self-pity feeds our pride and excuses the selfish attention it thrives on. Self-pity is never satisfied; because it is selfish, it demands more and more. There is only one true way to deal with self-pity, and that is to repent and ask God's forgiveness.

• • • • • •

Pray a simple prayer of repentance for the sin of pride and its fruit in Your life. I have often prayed words similar to these:

> Dear Lord,
> Please forgive me for my pride. I can't see my pride
> by myself, so I ask You to show me the fruit of my

pride. Help me to humble myself and acknowledge my sin to You and to others. Lord, I have taken my sin too lightly. Please convict me and reveal my heart to me. Help me to hate pride as You do. Help me to see how pride grieves You and hurts others. I will do anything You ask of me to be free from pride.

In your name, I pray. Amen.

Reflecting and Responding

1. Read through Philippians 2:2–7 and turn it into a prayer. Do a discovery Bible study on this passage.

2. How can pride be a form of stealing from God?

3. Describe how pride causes callousness to the needs of the poor.

4. What is the solution for pride?

5. What "fruit" of pride do you struggle with the most?

6. Reread the definition of pride at the beginning of the chapter, and then define the opposite of pride—humility.

SIX

Faithfulness

Recently a pastor named Ndaba Ndlovu came to speak to our students at Africa House, our All Nations training center in Cape Town. Ndaba started by saying that he wanted to talk about being "fat Christians." He spelled it out for us—F-A-T—then he wrote it on the whiteboard, and beside each letter wrote these words:

F—Faithful

A—Available

T—Teachable

The students at Africa House remembered Ndaba's talk long after he left! They joked with one another about getting FAT for Jesus. Though he shared in the humor, Ndaba was serious about being servant leaders who were faithful, available, and teachable. He shared his own journey of stepping down from a paid pastoral position to serve in the townships of South Africa. By going into disadvantaged communities without a grand title or a guaranteed salary, Ndaba lives out what he taught our leaders-in-training.

After traveling in twenty-six African countries for over thirty years, I have concluded that Africa is desperate for servant leaders. The same is true for America and the UK, and Europe and Australia. No form of leadership will be effective if it is not built on faithfulness and servanthood. The word *servant* has a particularly negative connotation in postcolonial Africa, but it is the right word. I use the term the way Jesus used it:

Jesus came to serve others, not to be served	Matthew 20:28
You cannot serve two masters	Matthew 6:24
To worship God alone	Luke 4:8
Greatness is found in serving	Matthew 23:11
Faithfulness to God is serving God	Matthew 24:40
To serve Jesus is to develop a life of intimacy with Jesus	John 15:4–5 (MSG)
Jesus wants His servants to be His friends	John 15:15
To serve the poor is to serve Jesus	Matthew 25:40

A servant who *works* for somebody earns a wage and has no choice but to do as he or she is told. But being a faithful servant in God's kingdom is voluntary; it is done out of love for Jesus. Servants of Jesus are not paid wages, but we are rewarded with friendship with Jesus. All service in the kingdom of God is rendered first to Jesus, then to others. When we serve the poor, we are serving Jesus. Jesus taught His disciples that when they served the poor and the most needy of people in His name, they did it for Him.

Where I live, there is a vast army of "generals" without many "servants." Pastors in Africa—both black and white—often model leadership as a top-down position, driving the best cars and bestowing grand titles on themselves. Meanwhile Africa suffers; Africans cry out for servants to help free them from corrupt officials, domineering government leaders, and even church pastors, as well as to be freed from the ravages of AIDS, malaria, and war.

Sub-Saharan Africa has been evangelized many times, but not discipled. Africa yearns for fully devoted disciples of Jesus who are not worried about titles, money from the West, status, positions, or success in man's eyes. There is a vast need for an army of servants who, instead of flaunting impressive-looking business cards showing their titles and honorary degrees, are men and women whose significance is found in the eyes of Jesus.

The tendency of many in Africa is to avoid the mundane and graduate to the spectacular, but that is not God's way. In Africa, a continent with more poverty than any other, the "prosperity teaching" coming out of America is enriching already fat and sassy so-called spiritual leaders. In contrast, godly character

It is in the realm of unseen servanthood that world-changers are made and trained.

is exemplified through faithfulness, availability, and teachableness, which may be seen as easily in small, humble tasks as in large, important-looking ones.

The best way to find out how we can serve God most effectively is by starting where we are, by doing the things no one else will do. Many of us have met people who claim they are called to do great things for God. However, while they are waiting for "great things" to start happening, they do nothing. They are unwilling to do anything "less" than their "calling." But that is not God's way; He wants us to start by being faithful in the small things, in the unseen world of servanthood.

How One Faithful Servant Transformed a Continent

It is in the realm of unseen servanthood that world-changers are made and trained. One such leader in history is Patrick of Ireland.[1]

Slavery and finding God

Patrick was sixteen years old when Irish raiders stormed his village in Roman Britain. Until that day, he had lived a privileged life. His grandfather was a priest and his father a magistrate and church leader. The raiders seized him and returned across the sea to the pagan land of Ireland, where they sold him into slavery. The year was 405 AD.

For the next six years, Patrick lived the lonely and hard life of a slave, working as a shepherd. Isolation, hunger, and cold brought Patrick much misery, and misery taught him humility. God worked powerfully in Patrick's suffering to remake him from the inside out, teaching him faithfulness and dependence on God alone.

Before his abduction, Patrick did not believe in God. Later he described how he turned to God when he realized God had been protecting him and loved him as a father loves his son.

Outwardly, nothing changed for Patrick; he was still a captive in a harsh foreign land, but he learned to see life differently. The land of his captivity had become the land of his freedom—in God.

The love of God grew in Patrick. He stayed out in the forests and on the mountains to pray at night and would rise before dawn to pray in the icy coldness of the Irish winter. This was a delight for him because the Spirit was burning in him.

Escape and return to Ireland

God revealed to Patrick in a dream that a ship was waiting to take him home. Patrick made his escape and began the long journey home as a runaway slave.

He reached the ship and eventually made it back to his family, resuming the life he once had in Britain. But God, who is the initiator in this story, had other plans for Patrick.

One night Patrick woke to hear the voices of the people he had known in Ireland crying out, "We beg you, come and walk with us again!" Their cry pierced his heart. God was calling him to return.

Patrick faced opposition from the church leaders, but he believed that God had appointed him to go to the Irish people. When he returned to Ireland, it had been four hundred years since Christ commanded His disciples to go to all the nations, yet the gospel was still largely contained within the borders of the Roman Empire. But God put within Patrick the faith of an apostle, compelling him by the Spirit to take the gospel to the ends of the earth. The shepherd-boy slave had become the slave of Christ and missionary to Ireland.

Patrick's troubles had prepared him well for his mission. His heart longed to reach the "barbarians" beyond the borders of civilization. Patrick did not have the training of the priests and leaders in the church, but his lack of formal training contributed to his openness to new and effective methods.

Transforming Europe

The Irish believed in a bewildering array of gods, goddesses, and spirits of the sky, earth, and water, as well as the magical powers of ancestors and animal sacrifices. Patrick saw the need and opportunity to reach these Irish barbarians. Despite fierce opposition from the Druids and violent local chieftans as well as the Roman church, he traveled to remote and dangerous places to preach, baptize converts, and train others to lead the new churches. Thousands turned from their pagan idols to serve the living God. Many of the converts took up Patrick's challenge to join his missionary movement.

Although Patrick was part of the Roman church, he lived and communicated the gospel in ways that connected and resonated deeply with Irish hopes and concerns, teaching the Irish that they could become followers of Christ without having to become like Romans.

Steadily the gospel worked its power through Irish tribal society. Patrick redeemed the best of tribal culture to serve the gospel and opposed the aspects that did not conform to the gospel. He ended the slave trade, and under the gospel's influence, murder and tribal warfare decreased. Patrick showed the Irish that it was possible to be brave, indeed to be warriors—but for Jesus and not against one another.

Pilgrim

The disciple-making movement led by Patrick was not a highly organized or centrally controlled operation. Wave after wave of Irish youth flooded into Christian service and lived lives devoted to God. Small communities of followers of Jesus responded to the call of Christ and gathered with others, committed to spiritual devotion as they served the poor. They were also "sending communities." For centuries afterward, Ireland became a base from which the good news of Jesus spread throughout the British Isles and much of western and northern Europe, as disciples of Jesus followed the call to "go on pilgrimage for Christ."

God wants to do the same today

God is preparing a movement of young revolutionaries today who are willing to lay down their lives to serve the poor of the earth as they make disciples for Jesus. I meet these young men and women everywhere I go—in Europe, the United States, Great Britain, and South Africa. I meet them in the townships and along the roadsides, in the universities and in farming communities.

Patrick's followers shared a love for Irish culture, but the Scriptures had first place in their hearts and minds. And there are disciples of Jesus today who appreciate their culture but love Jesus even more. They study God's Word with passion rather than detached academic interest and seek to engage their culture from the front lines of committed communities of faith.

Patrick's disciples were not great theologians, but they had spiritual devotion and zeal. Those who once would have given their lives in feuds between the clans and tribes in Ireland instead gave their lives to plant the gospel wherever Christ led them. To see the same today, you have only to turn up at large conventions of dedicated youth (e.g., Urbana, onething, Passion) or visit the training communities of youth movements like 24-7 Prayer, YWAM, and Young Life.

Young men and women in Ireland trained and sent by Patrick and his followers then recruited new disciples from the local people and sent them out to found new communities. More harvest workers were located in the harvest itself. Celtic mission communities became highly flexible, adaptable, and transplantable—everything that the church of the Roman Empire was not.

Patrick the faithful

Patrick's personal achievements were impressive, but his greater legacy was the missional movement he inspired through his fierce focus and faithfulness. The monasteries of the Celtic movement became dynamic training centers of spiritual devotion, learning, industry, and discipleship in a chaotic fifth-century world. There are many who share the same passion as Patrick, the faithful servant of Jesus. My wife and I and a band of friends started Africa House in Cape Town, where we impart vocational skills and passionate hearts to all who will devote themselves to follow Jesus wherever He leads. And the same is happening around the world through the movement we lead called All Nations. Matt and Elizabeth Chen are leading the way in Taiwan, as Mike and Dominic Ely are doing in Romania and Mary Ho, Pam Arlund, and Randy Catlett are doing in Kansas City.

As the number of Patrick's monasteries multiplied throughout Ireland, Britain, and the European continent, new missionaries were sent out to "go on pilgrimage for Christ" wherever they felt His leading. All it took for them was to be faithful to Jesus. The same happens among today's followers of Jesus. Each year, thousands of teams are sent from local churches to share Jesus in Africa, Asia, and Europe.

The movement continues

Patrick died in 461. As the western part of the Roman Empire crumbled and darkness spread over much of Europe, the light of the gospel shone brightly from remote Ireland. For the next five hundred years, the youth of Ireland and their disciples fanned out across Europe, winning converts, making disciples, and multiplying missionary outposts.

There is a similar movement in our world today. African civilization is being renewed across our continent by devout followers of Jesus. A movement in Europe refuses to yield to European cynicism. Korea, China, and India are experiencing massive movements to Christ, the largest and fastest growing in two thousand years of church history!

It is a spontaneous movement of the Spirit. There is not one "Patrick" in this movement, but thousands. From the mountains of southern Ethiopia to the universities of Korea; from the villages of north India to the student churches of South Africa; from fresh, new churches in the United States to the passionate movements of South America, God is raising up thousands of disciples across the globe who are joining God's mission to transform the world.

Are you a Patrick?

What is your role in this movement? Are you being equipped by God as His faithful servant? Will you break down barriers and spread the good news of the kingdom of God in a disadvantaged community somewhere close to you? Are you serving AIDS babies in Africa, or campaigning against sex trafficking in Asia?

Throughout the Bible, God gives to people promises of the great things He wants to do through them, but seldom are the promises fulfilled immediately. The process of bringing about change to a community in need is a long road of servanthood and faithfulness.

Our reward for faithfulness is not first from those we serve, but from the One who called us to serve.

Serve—*Now*

If you feel called to work with the poor, start where the need is. The disadvantaged communities near where you live are crying out for people who care enough to get involved—as are those of Africa! Our community is involved in two programs started by young men and women with a dream in their hearts to serve the poor. One young woman, Bethany O'Connor, had a burden on her heart to rescue abandoned children, and now she is living her dream, which she calls "Baby Safe." Missy, Sarah, and Jeremiah launched the other program, "Vulnerable Children," and work beside a local "Mama" named Wendy who has been caring for three hundred child-headed households for years, never asking for anything for herself. (A child-headed household is one where the parents have died of AIDS, leaving no caregivers to help the children.)

All that was needed were some ordinary followers of Jesus to stir up their courage, step out of their comfort zones, and get involved. If you don't know where to begin, write to me (details at the back of the book), and I will help you. Skill counts, but the greatest need is faithfulness, availability, and teachableness.

God wants to train you for the future—*now*. He wants to develop in you the character strength of humble faithfulness. Those who are unfaithful to God's call fall by the way. But those who hold on to God's promises, keeping alive the passion God kindles in their hearts—those are the ones who make a difference. In a world of great need, the greatest need of all is for people to follow Jesus the faithful servant. Servants of Jesus must be faithful; a self-seeking, "hit-and-run" type of servanthood can cause great heartache and disillusionment in those who are being served. Those who are faithful will win.

Three Kinds of Faithfulness

God gives us promises to inspire us, then follows a process of preparation for us. Jesus speaks about this process in Luke 16:10–12, where He clarifies three areas of character training that are essential for every faithful follower of Christ. Take time to think about and pray over the following three areas of faithfulness—pray that you will learn to love God faithfully.

Faithful with little

Jesus said,

> *Unless you are faithful in small matters, you won't be faithful in large ones. If you cheat even a little, you won't be honest with greater responsibilities. (Luke 16:10 NLT)*

In Matthew 25, Jesus tells a parable about faithfulness. A master gave each of his servants varying amounts of money before leaving on a long trip. They did not all receive the same amount of money, in much the same way as we all have differing levels of skill and ability.

Upon his return, the master inquired as to what his servants had done with the money he had given them. He discovered that the first two servants had invested the money wisely and now had twice as much. The third, however, had buried his money and had only the amount the master had given him.

Jesus drew an interesting conclusion from this: "For everyone who has will be given more, and he will have an abundance. Whoever does not have, even what he has will be taken from him" (Matt. 25:29). Although this passage speaks of wise stewardship over money, the principle applies to every area of life.

If we discipline ourselves by taking care of what we have at hand, we will be laying character foundations for God to trust us with much more. What do you "have" that you are not taking care of? Could you take the initiative to do something to show yourself faithful? In everyday tasks, such as cleaning, showing up to work on time, not cheating on income taxes, giving tithes and offerings as God leads us, we need to show ourselves faithful in little. Show me a person who is not disciplined in the little things of life, and I will show you a person who is not ready for more spiritual responsibility. Faithfulness in little is the fruit of loving Jesus in the things that are important to Him. If He cannot trust us with the small, seemingly unimportant details, we are not the kind of people who can be trusted with greater responsibility.

Faithful with material things

> And if you are untrustworthy about worldly wealth,
> who will trust you with the true riches of heaven?
> (Luke 16:11 NLT)

If we are to be used by God in serving people, we must learn to be faithful with "things." Through our diligence and reliability with material things—whether money, books, cars, bicycles, clothes, or anything else—we demonstrate to God, and to others, that we can be counted on. We show, by being faithful, that we are serious about loving God.

The word that is used for material things in Luke 16 is *mammon*. It translates as "riches" and, more particularly, "the material things that riches can buy." Are we faithful over the things we have? Some believe "earthly things" are not an important part of loving God. But in many ways, handling money and "things" is preparation for spiritual responsibilities. If we are to prove ourselves faithful, we will handle material possessions wisely, not selfishly.

Many leaders involved in the training of new leaders observe emerging leaders to see if they are faithful. If they cannot be good stewards with things, how can they be trusted to care for people? If they are rushing to make money and protect possessions, how can they hear God telling them to lay down their lives for others?

We need to examine ourselves very carefully: Do we pay our bills on time and are we taking steps to stay out of debt? Are we scrupulously honest with our taxes? Are we faithful in the tasks assigned to us by others? These life situations are God's testing grounds to see if we are ready for greater responsibility in His kingdom.

Faithful in what belongs to others

> *And if you have not been faithful in that which is*
> *another's, who will give you that which is your own?*
> *(Luke 16:12 RSV)*

It is easy to get "spiritual" when considering the will of God, but this verse puts things on a very practical level. Are we faithful with possessions that belong to other people? Or do we borrow things and not return them? Are we more careless with others' possessions than we are with our own? Do we give our employers our best, or are we lax on the job, leaving early when they are not around? If we are not faithful in these areas, why do we suppose God will give us bigger tasks and more authority?

Let's take this truth and apply it to submission and accountability to serving spiritual leaders. Read the passage again in the light of serving in a church, church-planting effort, or ministry to the poor: "And if you have not been faithful in another person's *church or ministry*, who will give you your own?" The most effective pastors and spiritual leaders around the world today did not start out with high-profile ministries but began by serving someone else. As they proved themselves and demonstrated that they could be trusted to undertake and complete a task, they were recognized and given more responsibility. This is the biblical model: Prove yourself capable of serving another person, serve the ministry or church of another, show yourself trustworthy in the small things, and God will give you your own—not as a reward, but because you have learned to put others above yourself.

Biblical Examples of Faithfulness

Joseph

The life of Joseph provides a picture of this truth at work. God gave Joseph a promise that his brothers would serve him. However, Joseph had much character development in store before he was ready for the fulfillment of that promise. Being sold into slavery by his brothers certainly didn't seem like a step toward ruling over them!

Eventually he found himself in an Egyptian jail, where he spent a lot of time wondering what had gone wrong. As God tested and prepared Joseph, Joseph proved himself faithful and was given a greater task with greater authority. Joseph ended up doing, on a large scale, exactly what he had proven himself faithful in doing while in jail: overseeing people and resources. Through faithfulness he proved he was ready for the promise's fulfillment, and his brothers did bow before him and serve him as God had shown him (Gen. 37—47).

The story of Joseph is a reminder that if you serve under controlling leaders, God will release you if you are faithful. No leader can keep you from the will of God if you walk humbly with Him. God is committed to getting each of us into the place He has for us!

Saul

God made promises to Saul, Israel's first king. By appointing Saul, God was inviting him to learn to be faithful. But Saul's character could not sustain the responsibility God entrusted to him. Despite repeated opportunities to prove himself and grow on the job, he continually made poor choices. Eventually God removed Saul as king and gave David authority and blessing instead. When God opens a door of opportunity for us, just as He did for Saul, *a test always accompanies the opportunity.* Leadership assignments from God are not guarantees of a

A position of leadership may only compound areas of weakness in our character if we don't learn the lessons God has for us.

cozy position, power, entitlement, and influence, but they are invitations to learn new levels of servanthood.

Many think that once they get a position of responsibility, God will somehow anoint them with His Spirit and cover their weaknesses. The story of Saul, however, illustrates that this doesn't work. God gave Saul a leadership position but required him to walk in humility before God and others. A position of leadership may only compound areas of weakness in our character if we don't learn the lessons God has for us. We should deal with them in the present, lest they cause much heartache and embarrassment in the future. If a leadership appointment reveals weaknesses in our lives, then we must humble ourselves before God, those we work with, and possibly also those we lead, acknowledging our weakness and asking for help.

David

David knew that God had called him to be king, but he did not seek kingship. Instead, he trusted God to bring it about. On several occasions, David had an opportunity to kill Saul and claim the position God promised him, but he did not. He wanted it in God's way and time, and eventually his patience and faithfulness were rewarded.

Faithfulness is like the hinge on a door. It is only a small thing, yet without it even the largest of doors will not open.

After David became king, character weaknesses were exposed in his life as well. The difference between Saul and David was that David repented and acknowledged his weaknesses, and Saul did not.

Your Commitment to Faithfulness

God's promises are never an excuse to ride over others in pursuit of His will. He will fulfill His word to us in time if we are faithful where we are now. We dare not attempt to avoid testing and proving.

Perhaps a test of our commitment to servanthood and faithfulness is our readiness to pray a prayer like the following. Read it carefully. If you are prepared to make this commitment to grow in faithfulness, make it your own.

> Father, I'll do things Your way. I trust You to bring about Your purposes in my life, in Your time and Your way. Do everything You need to do in me to prepare me, Father. Test me and teach me to be the faithful person You want me to be. I will not take shortcuts to Your promises in my life. As You show me the things You want to change in me, I will learn them, with Your help and grace, as I submit to You and others You put over me. Amen.

Faithfulness is like the hinge on a door. It is only a small thing, yet without it even the largest of doors will not open. By being faithful now, we make a hinge on which God can swing the door wide open for us in the future.

Don't miss the hinge by looking for the wrong door! Get ready now: Become a faithful follower of Jesus.

Reflecting and Responding

1. Do a discovery Bible study on 1 Corinthians 4:15–17.

2. What kinds of responsibilities do you have now, and are you fulfilling them faithfully? Make a list of the areas where God is testing you and teaching you to be faithful in little, in material things, and in what belongs to others.

3. How would you evaluate your faithfulness with finances? For example, do you repay loans? Do you budget and plan ahead? Are you generous to others? Do you stay out of debt? And are you living free from the love of "things"?

4. Can you freely serve a ministry and vision God has given to others? Go to those who supervise or oversee you at work or at church, and ask them for an honest evaluation of how you can improve in your "faithfulness" to them.

SEVEN

Prayer

The story is told about one of the finest and wisest Christians in the sixteenth century, Philip Neri, who was asked by the pope to travel to a convent near Rome and meet a certain novice who was reputed to be a saint. Neri rode on his mule, through the mud and the mire of country roads in the winter, to reach the convent. Arriving there, he asked for the novice. When she entered the room, he asked her to take off his boots, which were caked in mud from the long journey. She refused to do such a menial task, affronted at the very idea that she, with her reputation, should be asked to do this.

Neri said no more. He left the convent and went back to Rome. "Don't wonder any longer," he said to the pope. "Here is no saint, for here is no humility.'

The Humility of Prayer

If the epitome of pride is self-centeredness, then the epitome of humility is prayer. In coming to earth in the form of servant, Jesus took the initiative to come near to us. In doing so, He invites us to come near to Him. How do we do this? There is no greater way to draw near to Jesus than spending time with Him in prayer.

Learning from Jesus

To learn from Jesus in prayer is to embrace humility. Those who are too busy to spend time with Jesus alone in prayer are too proud to learn from Him. We learn from Jesus by spending time in His presence and by reading His teachings in the New Testament and applying them to our lives.

Becoming like Jesus

We will not become like Jesus without prayer. The goal of prayer is to become like Jesus—for the sake of others. To pursue knowing and becoming like Jesus requires time alone with Him.

> **To learn from Jesus in prayer is to embrace humility. Those who are too busy to spend time with Jesus … are too proud to learn from Him.**

Depending on Jesus

Dependence on Jesus involves acknowledging our need of Him. We must daily look to Jesus as a friend, as the one true source of wisdom. Jesus gives counsel and direction in every important decision of our lives.

Developing a deep relationship with Jesus

People who do not know God are deeply aware that something is missing. When they discover that God loves them and offers forgiveness, they experience a longing to go deeper and know more.

Without prayer, our service for God and others may satisfy us for a period of time, but there comes a moment when our souls cry out for more. Do you tend to substitute form for reality, action for relationship, and busyness for communion? Prayer is how you demonstrate that you will no longer substitute *doing* for *being*, or religious fervor for spiritual reality. Prayer takes you beyond religion to Jesus Himself. No religious form or symbol can, in the end, be a substitute for a personal encounter with Jesus in the place of private prayer.

Saying yes to Jesus' plan for our lives

There will be many times you will be tempted to negotiate with Jesus concerning His will for your life. The temptation is to find out what He wants from us, then decide if we like it. But prayers of humility give us the opportunity to say yes to His will for our lives.

Being known by Jesus for who we really are

We live in a world that rewards superficiality and encourages covering up weaknesses, wounds, and secret sins. But Jesus is the epitome of truthfulness. To believe the truth about Jesus but to flee from truth in my own heart is to live a lie. Transparent prayers of baring your soul to Jesus free you to receive truth and grace from Him. There is no true doctrine apart from humility before God in prayer.

Going into the world Jesus made and loves

True spirituality leads us to engage in our Father's world. To be close to Jesus is to care about the world that was created through

Him and that He died to redeem. A passionate, personal prayer relationship with Jesus will inevitably lead us into the world that He cares so deeply about. Jesus demonstrated what He is passionate for when He died on the cross for the sins of the whole world. Has your prayer led you to share His passion? Our passion for the world is a measure of our passion for Jesus.

Cultivating Humility in Prayer

When I write about humility, I am not referring to a quality of life to be developed by a privileged "holy" few. All followers of Jesus who take their commitment to Jesus seriously recognize the great need to cultivate this virtue. Our integrity as followers of Jesus hinges on our response to the invitation to humble ourselves.

We are taught in the Bible that a humble pursuit of Jesus affects every area of life. To the first-century believers, Paul wrote these things:

> Be humble and gentle. Be patient with each other, making allowance for each other's faults because of your love. Always keep yourselves united in the Holy Spirit, and bind yourselves together with peace. (Eph. 4:2–3 NLT)

> Don't be selfish; don't live to make a good impression on others. Be humble, thinking of others as better than yourself. Don't think only about your own affairs, but be interested in others, too, and what they are doing. (Phil. 2:3–4 NLT)

Since God chose you to be the holy people whom he loves, you must clothe yourselves with tenderhearted mercy, kindness, humility, gentleness, and patience. You must make allowance for each other's faults and forgive the person who offends you. Remember, the Lord forgave you, so you must forgive others. (Col. 3:12–13 NLT)

Focusing on Jesus

In Romans chapters 7 and 8, Paul focuses on the self-centeredness of the worldly person and the willingness of the spiritual person to focus his or her life on Jesus. Chapter 7 of Romans is about the person who is living a self-centered life, and

We can focus wholeheartedly on only one person at a time—on ourselves or Jesus.

the battle that person has to live without guilt, shame, or condemnation. Worldly people are preoccupied with self. They are the center of their own universe. Indeed, the word *I* is used twenty-five times in this chapter! By contrast, *I* is used only twice in the description of the spiritual person in chapter 8. We can focus wholeheartedly on only one person at a time—on ourselves or Jesus.

By choosing to focus on Jesus, we are freed from preoccupation with ourselves. Conversely, pride holds us prisoner to self-centeredness, self-pity, self-love, self-sufficiency, self-infatuation, and self-indulgence. Humility frees us from this wretched state and allows us to enjoy God and to love others in a way proud people cannot (Col. 3:12–14).

Seven Prayer Exercises

I would like to do the rest of the chapter differently. I would like to guide you through a few simple prayer exercises to encourage and help you practically. Instead of merely writing about loving Jesus through spending time with Him, let's actually do it. Many people I talk to aspire to pray more but don't know how to take practical steps to put that aspiration into action. If not all of these exercises work for you, don't worry about it. See them as spiritual tools to help you build a prayer life. I use all of them at different times, some more than others. You can do these prayer exercises one after another as you read the chapter, or you can review them and then spread them out over a week. Or preferably, do both.

Over the years I have added to my spiritual toolbox by watching and learning from how others pray. If you want to dig deeper into prayer, I encourage you to read *Secrets of the Secret Place* by Bob Sorge and *God on Mute* by Pete Greig.[1]

Praying behind closed doors

> *But when you pray, go away by yourself, shut the door behind you, and pray to your Father secretly. Then your Father, who knows all secrets, will reward you. (Matt. 6:6 NLT)*

Find a room or a place somewhere you can be totally alone for a minimum of fifteen minutes to a half hour. The idea is to find a quiet, secluded place so you won't be distracted—or tempted to pray in order to impress others. Go into that room and shut the door.

When the door clicks behind you, believe in your heart that you will enter the presence of God. This is God's promise to us. Just be there in silence in God's presence; then after some time spent quieting your heart, begin to speak to Him as simply and honestly as you can.

After you shut the door, every distracting thought becomes a subject of prayer. Pray about every thought that comes to mind. Instead of battling to pray, you will have a wide array of thoughts to pray about. As you exhaust your natural thoughts, let your focus shift to God Himself, and you will begin to sense His grace. Pour out your heart and mind to Him. Tell Him what you are thinking about, what you are longing for, what you desire to happen. Tell Him about the cares of the day and the relationships in your life … whatever comes to mind.

Now, begin to thank Him. Thank Him for who He is, then thank Him for what He has done for you. Dedicate your life to Him by praying through aspects of your physical makeup: Dedicate **your mind**—what you think and the decisions you make; **your eyes**—what you see and how you look at things; **your tongue**—how you speak, what you say to others; **your ears**—what you listen to; **your hands**—what you do; **your feet**—where you go. When you are finished, listen quietly to the still, small voice inside and see if He has anything to say to you.

Meditate on the verse from Matthew 6 at the top of this section, written for our encouragement. This is the secret of the secret place; this is the guaranteed way to be in God's presence: The Father is already in the secret place, waiting for you. He has gone ahead of you; He is waiting for you. All you have to do to find Him is to go in to a quiet place and shut the door.

Praying the Disciple's Prayer

Take time to pray through the Disciple's Prayer (known to many as the Lord's Prayer), alone. Sit or kneel and pray through it phrase by phrase, taking time to expand in your own words what each phrase stands for. As you pray each part of the prayer, think creatively about what words you can use to expand the prayer to speak to the Father from your heart. For example, when I pray, "Our Father in heaven," I tell God how special He is to me as my Father. I ask Him to reveal His Father love to me deep within my heart. I speak to Him about His greatness and His goodness—He is my Father who loves and watches over me.

I continue to pray the Disciple's Prayer phrase by phrase, expanding on each phrase. Jesus knew what He was doing when He taught the disciples to pray this prayer. It is a guide for praying; a way to pray that fills our time with Jesus with new meaning.

Note that each part of the prayer represents an important aspect of our relationship with God. We need each element of the Disciple's Prayer as part of our daily relationship with Jesus, if we are to grow and be sensitive to the Holy Spirit. We need to worship Him, to be consecrated to Him, to confess our weakness to Him, to receive His empowering, to fight the Enemy in spiritual warfare, and to make ourselves available to serve Him. Through the Disciple's Prayer, we are empowered to *follow*.

I was taught to pray the Disciple's Prayer by a mentor who discipled me more than forty years ago. I still pray this prayer almost every day. You can pray through it in five minutes or for much longer. Go ahead and pray it now.

- **Worship**—*Our Father in heaven.* Worship God as our loving Father. Declare to Him your love and trust in His goodness, His mercy, and His greatness.

- **Consecration**—*Holy be Your name.* Ask God to show you areas of your life where He wants you to be holy. Dedicate yourself to Him. To consecrate something is to set it aside, so set aside every part of your life for Him.

- **Intercession**—*Your kingdom come. Your will be done on earth as it is in heaven.* Make a list of a few people or places where you want God to bring a little bit of heaven to earth—then ask Him. Ask Him to bring His kingdom, His rule, to people's hearts and minds. Name those people to the Lord.

- **Holy Spirit empowering**—*Give us this day our daily bread.* Ask God to fill you with all you need, especially the Holy Spirit; yield your life to Him to be like Jesus.

- **Confession and forgiveness**—*And forgive us our debts, as we forgive our debtors.* Ask for forgiveness for anything that you know has hurt people or grieved God. Receive His forgiveness.

- **Spiritual warfare**—*And do not lead us into temptation, but deliver us from evil.* Consciously turn away from evil around you, in your thoughts and actions. The Enemy attacks us with accusations, temptations, and deception. Pray against all three.

- **Commissioning to His service**—*For Yours is the kingdom and the power and the glory forever. Amen.* Make yourself totally available to do anything God asks of you to make Jesus known.

Praying through listening

> *When they drag you into their meeting places, or into*
> *police courts and before judges, don't worry about*
> *defending yourselves—what you'll say or how you'll*
> *say it.… The Holy Spirit will give you the right words*
> *when the time comes. (Luke 12:11–12 MSG)*

The exciting thing about this prayer exercise is that it can hap-pen anytime and anywhere—after you "shut the door" in your secret place, when you are walking across the street, at work or school, in your neighborhood, or while you are walking to a shop. We will do some specific practicing, but remember that listening prayer is a lifestyle.

At the beginning of each day, ask God to speak to you anytime during the day. Tell Him you are available and you will obey Him. You may feel fear about what He may ask you to do, but remember, faith is not the absence of fear but courage in the face of fear. God will give you faith and courage to do the thing He asks you to do.

There are different ways in which to do "listening prayer." For example, ask the Father to give you a special message for someone during the day or to tell you to do something for somebody. When He tells you, obey Him, there and then. If you cannot do it immedi-ately, make a note or a plan to follow through.

My friend Keith Tallman had a good paying job in California. Life was going well. Then one day, as he listened in prayer, the Father told Keith to quit his job and take a lesser-paying job. It would mean taking a significant pay cut and perhaps losing his house. Keith asked

God to confirm that he was really hearing Him. God sent people, out of the blue, to Keith and his wife with specific messages from God that Keith was to change jobs.

Keith obeyed, sensing in his heart that someone needed him at the new company where he was to work. And, true enough, the first week on the new job a man told Keith, "I have been praying that God would send someone to me here at work. I'm desperate for God." The man came to faith in Jesus, and like the story of the Philippian jailer in the book of Acts, his whole household did as well.

Was it worthwhile, giving up a job to reach one family for Jesus? That depends on your values, your "real beliefs." If you love God and give Him everything, and you ask to hear the Holy Spirit and He answers you, then your obedience to Him is worth far more than money or job security. Will you obey God if He speaks to you?

Here is another story to encourage this kind of prayer: A student named A. J. was walking across his campus when he saw a girl named Angela with her arms covered by the sleeves of a long-sleeved T-shirt. A. J. tells the story best in his own words: "I heard a little voice in my head saying, 'Ask her to show you her arms.' I figured it was the Holy Spirit so I went up to her and asked her if I could see her arms."

She said, "Who told you?" A. J. persisted and asked to see her arms. She finally agreed, raised her sleeves—and there were two large Xs carved in her arms. "Who told you about my arms?" she persisted. A. J. answered, "God told me, Angela. He loves you, and He doesn't want you to do that to yourself." This encounter eventually led to

Angela's coming to faith in Jesus, and ultimately Angela became a missionary.[2]

To practice listening prayer, get alone with God, "shut the door," quiet your heart by singing or listening to a worship song, then kneel or sit quietly and ask God to speak to you. Write down what you hear in response to three specific questions:

1. Ask God one thing He wants to say about His love for you personally.
2. Ask God one thing He wants to say about your neighbors or family and how you're to serve them.
3. Ask God one thing He wants to say about reaching out to someone in need.

Write down the things God tells you to do or to pray about, then follow through with them. But don't stop with that one time of prayer—practice being quiet inside and listen at different times through your day. Actively ask God to speak to you through impressions or thoughts about a neighbor, a friend, someone at work or at school or on your bus, train, or taxi.

Some friends of mine call this "treasure hunting." Because God looks upon every human being as a treasure, when we listen to Him, we are allowing God to take us with Him through listening prayer on "treasure hunts." Continue this practice all week. Follow your impressions. Make note of the times it did not work out and the times it did. Learning to listen to God's voice is a journey. Don't give up if it doesn't go well the first time. It's like learning to ride a bike— you'll get better as you practice!

PRAYER   129

Praying through journaling

To those who are open to my teaching, more understanding will be given. But to those who are not listening, even what they have will be taken away from them. (Mark 4:25 NLT)

In these verses, Jesus teaches His disciples to hold on to what He taught them, especially if they wanted to receive more. *It is important,* Jesus says, *so remember what I'm teaching you—even write it down!* Which they did, of course. That is how we have the New Testament. Matthew, Mark, John, Peter, and James—as well as Luke, Paul, and others—all wrote down what Jesus taught them.

If God said only one thing to you throughout your whole life, you would not struggle to remember it; but He wants to speak to you more than once. But He won't keep speaking to you if you don't take it seriously. Record what He teaches you with the date in a notebook or journal or in a special folder on your computer. I write my journal on my iPhone, on my laptop, and in a notebook. It's too important to forget anything He tells you. While writing things down doesn't equate to remembering them, it certainly goes a long way toward it. I write in my journal when I am angry or confused and when I am deeply moved by the Holy Spirit. I turn my thoughts into prayers of request to God. I write down things I think God may be promising me, or dreams or ideas of things I think He wants me to do. Recording my prayers in my journal helps me clear my thoughts and gives more depth to my prayers. I have to think through the words I use when I write them down.

I keep a journal when I pray, especially when I want to remember something important from listening prayer or a discovery Bible study. I have learned that if I want to learn more from God, I have to record, to remember what He was teaching me. These lessons usually come to me as impressions in my mind. I write them down and review them from time to time. I don't write in my journal every day, but as I need to.

In Jesus' words in Mark 4, we learn that God might actually take things from us if we don't take them seriously and act on them. To apply this lesson to prayer, I encourage you to write down the things God tells you or teaches you. Record questions about the decisions you must make and then, as God speaks, record His answers. Write prayers to God. You can try this right now. Get in a quiet place and journal a simple prayer to God. Tell Him what you want to learn from Him.

Prayer is talking to God. It is not *something to do;* it is *someone to talk to.* It can be both silent and spoken, written and verbal. Prayer is an expression from the heart to Jesus. Journaling prayer not only will help you remember what you want to say to God and what He says to you but will also help you to be accountable to God. God expects us to obey Him. Prayer is not only for friendship and worship, but also for instruction and direction. God gives us assignments in prayer. Let's be those who are practiced in remembering what God says to us.

Praying the Scriptures

Many years ago, a friend and I decided to share our prayer times with Jesus together each morning. The first morning my friend opened his Bible and invited me to pray with him through the Psalms. It was the first time I had heard of turning Bible passages into prayers. It has become a way of life for me since that time.

Some followers of Jesus say they get bored with prayer, or don't know what to pray about, or find that they are easily distracted. The solution? Pray the Bible.

I go through the Psalms and turn every verse that is praising God or declaring His greatness into a prayer of personal worship. I underline the verses and go back through them repeatedly, using them as prayers. Another way I pray the Scriptures—one of my favorites—is to pray Paul's prayers. In most of his letters, he tells the new believers that he prays for them, then gives them a few sentences about how he prays for them. There is great wisdom and depth in those prayers.

Here is one example from Paul's letter to the Philippians:

> Every time I think of you, I give thanks to my God. I always pray for you, and I make my requests with a heart full of joy because you have been my partners in spreading the Good News about Christ from the time you first heard it until now. And I am sure that God, who began the good work within you, will continue his work until it is finally finished on that day when Christ Jesus comes back again. It is right that I should feel as I do about all of you, for you have a very special place in my heart. We have shared together the blessings of God, both when I was in prison and when I was out, defending the truth and telling others the Good News. (Phil. 1:3–7 NLT)

Go through this prayer again and pray it for some of your friends, especially any you have helped come to faith in Jesus.

The Bible is one huge prayer book! Praying God's Word back to Him is powerful for several reasons:

- We are praying truth (Heb. 4:12).
- We are praying with substance and depth (Ps. 5:1; 12:6).
- We are praying with confidence (1 John 5:15).
- We are praying according to God's will (Ps. 119:11).

To practice this form of prayer, get into a quiet place, take your Bible, and turn to Psalm 67. Pray this psalm for the community or group of which you are a part. Now turn to Paul's prayer for the Thessalonians in 1 Thessalonians 1:2–5 and pray these words for those you want to come to faith in Jesus. You can pray the remainder of the chapter if you wish—it is filled with treasures! Try praying the Scriptures each time you are in a group prayer meeting. It will be much more meaningful to you.

Praying to express love for Jesus

This is the prayer of affection, of telling Jesus how much you love Him and are grateful to Him. This prayer is about telling Him you love who He is, what He has done for you, and how much He means to you.

Try it right now. Perhaps it is easy for you and you have practiced it many times, but if it is new to you, this is a great opportunity to develop words, expressions, and phrases of appreciation intentionally. What do you love about Jesus? Respect about Him? What are

you grateful to Him for? Tell Him! To help me do this I use Ephesians
1:3—2:10. Paul begins this passage by saying we are blessed with
every spiritual blessing in Christ, and then he describes those blessings. I turn those descriptions into prayers of thanksgiving.

Jesus loves to hear how much we admire Him. He never grows
tired of hearing our admiration and adoration. Take time to tell Him
why you respect, admire, appreciate, revere, and love Him.

Perhaps you need to spend more time in getting to know Jesus by
reading the gospel accounts of His life and teaching. I am reading the
gospel of Luke now, over and over again, slowly studying it, praying
through it, recording my impressions, and learning to love and appreciate Jesus more. I am reading Luke's gospel with the goal of learning
about Jesus. I have broken it down into topics that help me focus: the
things Jesus did for others, the wise things He taught, the questions
He asked, and how He trained His leaders. I have done studies on the
questions Jesus asked in Luke's gospel, the prayers He prayed and what
He taught about prayer, and the things He taught about discipleship.

Luke 20—24 is the story of the last week of Jesus' life, death on
the cross, resurrection, and the days following. These five chapters
describe what happened in the last eight days of His life, and then,
after the resurrection, what happened in the last few weeks of His time
on earth. I have turned the events of the last week before His death
into spontaneous prayers of intercession, worship, and consecration of
my life to Him. I encourage you to do the same.

Be captivated by Jesus. Don't try to come up with great prayers;
just love Him from your heart. Don't try to be a theologian—just be
real and honest and speak to Him about your relationship with Him
or the relationship you want to have with Him.

Praying to intercede

Intercession is prayer offered to God for the needs of others. To intercede is to go between, to plead for someone who is in need.

The writer of the letter to the Hebrews asked the believers to intercede on his behalf: "Pray for us, for our conscience is clear and we want to live honourably in everything we do. I especially need your prayers right now so that I can come back to you soon" (Heb. 13:18–19 NLT). The writer believed that if the people prayed for him, he would get to see them sooner. We can delay or speed up answers to prayer through our intercession. Our prayers make a difference, not just in us as we pray, but in people's circumstances. God will do what He has purposed to do, but He allows us to participate with Him in when and how things happen.

Jeremiah quoted what God promised him concerning this great prayer partnership: "Call to Me, and I will answer you, and show you great and mighty things, which you do not know" (Jer. 33:3 NKJV).

There are several ways you can be faithful as an intercessor. Keep a prayer list of people you want to pray for, or divide up your prayer list by topics and spread them out over a week, praying for a different topic each day. For example, pray for government leaders on Monday, family members on Tuesday, people at work on Wednesday, friends and neighbors on Thursday, countries and people groups that have never heard the good news of Jesus on Friday, people you are desiring to come to faith in Jesus on Saturday, and local churches on Sunday.

I suggest you take time now and practice this kind of prayer. Ask God to teach you to be an intercessor. Set aside time in your daily schedule to practice intercessory prayer. The Bible teaches us that Jesus intercedes for us (Rom. 8:27–34), so by learning to be an intercessor, we are drawing closer to Jesus Himself.

Reflecting and Responding

1. Do a discovery Bible study on Luke 18:1–8.

2. Write out a personal prayer to Jesus. Express in words your love and appreciation for who He is and what He has done for you.

3. Review the definition of humility and reflect on your relationship with Jesus using the definition as a guide. Compose a prayer of humility before the Lord.

4. Which of the seven ways to spend time with Jesus are you most comfortable with? Which way can you most likely grow in, and why do you think you would benefit from praying this way?

Part Two

LOVING THOSE WHO
DON'T KNOW JESUS

EIGHT

Practicing Jesus

Recently I drove to a hillside overlooking a settlement called Ocean View, deep in the southern suburbs of Cape Town. Set on the side of a mountain with spectacular views of the Atlantic, Ocean View offers outward beauty, but it carries inward pain. It is one of the communities in South Africa that was created by the forced removal of people of color from their homes in the 1960s because of race classification. Ocean View is a "Colored" community (the term Colored is the politically correct term, more importantly, the term the Colored people use to describe themselves). The Colored people of South Africa are descendants of the Khoisan, the original South Africans. The Khoisan were cattle herders in the Cape when the first European explorers arrived in the fifteenth century.

I am a recent arrival to South Africa, and although I visited South Africa many times during the apartheid years, I can't possibly understand what it's like to be forcibly removed from your home and ordered to move to a new, designated settlement a few kilometers down the road. The houses, meager dwellings compared to what they left behind, were perched on an inhospitable, windswept hillside, far away from shops and schools.

The Colored community of Ocean View was totally dislocated, suffering great shame and loss of identity. As I sat above Ocean View, I tried to imagine: What is it like to go past your old home, which was taken away from you, on your way to work? Or to buy groceries at the local supermarket, knowing that you are not wanted—or indeed, not allowed to live—in your former neighborhood? What do people feel when they think about their homes having been taken from them, simply because their skin had been the "wrong" color?

I sat in my pickup truck above Ocean View and looked down on the community and prayed. I asked God how I should intercede for these people. I experienced a great sadness as the Father reminded me of the deep rejection that resides in the "soul" of the community. I felt a deep grief, like what it must feel to be an orphan and have no place to belong … no family or mother or father to want you. So I prayed for acceptance and love to pervade the community. I pleaded with God to remove the cloud of shame that hangs over the community and to put a spirit of pride and dignity and belonging into the hearts of the men and women of Ocean View.

I was particularly moved to pray for the men of Ocean View. Since my arrival in South Africa, I have met some great men in the community who are setting good examples as husbands and fathers. But sadly, many men in the community are prisoners of alcohol and drugs, and still others are filled with anger and hopelessness. Crime is pervasive, and abuse is the secret sin that robs men of their confidence. So I prayed for the men of Ocean View to find their true hearts so they could walk with dignity. I prayed for the curse of drug addiction and alcoholism to be removed from the community, and for good men to be raised up.

The next afternoon I was back in Ocean View visiting Cedric and Sylvia Present. They are part of All Nations. Cedric and Sylvia live in a humble home, but they are proud of it and are doing a little bit each month to make improvements. They showed me the recent additions, and I rejoiced with them at God's provision.

Then Cedric pointed to the street outside and told me a story. Some local youngsters were causing trouble—throwing rocks on roofs, breaking windows, stealing, fighting, and buying and selling drugs. They have kept the neighbors awake at night and made people afraid to go out during the day. Finally, some of the men in the neighborhood decided take action. They used Cedric's house for a council of war. Cedric asked if he could open in prayer. God used Cedric to calm the people, to speak wisdom and peace to people's hearts. But Cedric didn't stop there.

Cedric followed up by meeting with the young guys hanging out on the street. He told them his story of coming to faith in Jesus and asked them if they would like to go with him sometime to visit one of the local prisons. The prison talk got their attention, and Cedric's story aroused their spiritual interest. And the young men felt respected because one of the older men took time to listen to them and speak from his heart.

As I drove away, it occurred to me that Cedric is a "man of peace" on his street. God has given him favor with both the older men and the young gang members. I thought of Jesus' words in Luke 10 when He spoke to His disciples as He was sending them off on a mission: "Whenever you visit someone in their home, speak a blessing over their home. If your blessing is received, those are people you should pay attention to. Visit more often and try to discern if these are people who are seeking God. Perhaps they are crying out for answers and will not only open their home to you, but their relationships as well" (vv. 5–7, author's paraphrase).

Jesus sent His disciples to preach the good news and told them that they should try to stay in homes of people who were open to them and their message. These are the people who often have influence in their neighborhoods or networks of relationships. I realized I didn't need to look any further to have access to this community—Cedric and Sylvia are there, "practicing Jesus."

Practicing Jesus Today

I heard a friend say recently that she was practicing Luke 10. She was referring to the principles Jesus taught His disciples before He sent them ahead of Him to heal the sick and announce the arrival of His kingdom. I thought about what it means to "practice" something. The dictionary defines *practice* as "doing something repeatedly in order to improve; doing something as an established custom or habit." If that is what it means to practice, then perhaps what we should "practice" more than anything else is Jesus. Instead of thinking about what new course we will do, or what program we will start, we should think about Jesus.

There is a "Jesus deficit disorder" in the church today. The person of Jesus has been replaced with great enthusiasm for "justice and reconciliation," "discipling the nations," "leadership principles," "core values,"

There is a "Jesus deficit disorder" in the church today.

and the "kingdom of God." I heard one church leader say recently that he was not interested in the "gospel of salvation" but only in the "gospel of the kingdom." I didn't understand the distinction between the two, but what stood out to me was the absence of Jesus from his language and his passion.

Len Sweet and Frank Viola recently made this statement about the "Jesus deficit disorder":

> What is Christianity? *It is Christ.* Nothing more. Nothing less. Christianity is not an ideology. Christianity is not a philosophy.… Conversion is more than a change in direction; it's a change in connection.[1]

What does practicing Jesus look like?[2]

What Does *Practicing Jesus* Mean Practically?

- We focus on the person of Jesus. We cannot separate the teachings of Jesus from the person of Jesus. Jesus is the message: the embodiment of the Sermon on the Mount and the essence of the kingdom of God.

- We make Jesus known so He can be loved and obeyed. God's greatest priority is not transformation of society, justice, healing, miracles, church growth, church planting, house church, missions, recovery, Bible study, discipleship, or anything else—just … *Jesus.* To quote Viola and Sweet, "He is the heart and bloodstream of God's plan. To miss this is to miss the plot."[3] All the other things are profoundly important— but only if the person of Jesus is central in everything.

- We don't simply imitate how Jesus lived, but choose to "be Jesus." We can do this with confidence, not because of who we are, but because of who He is in us.
- We don't ask, "What would Jesus do?" but, "What is He doing—now, in and through me?"
- We focus on the person of Christ, not the cause of Christ. Focusing on His cause or mission doesn't mean we are in fact *following Jesus.*
- We continually put ourselves on the cross in our hearts and ask Jesus to take the throne. We die to the selfish nature that wants to be in control of ourselves and others and ask Jesus to be in control.
- We practice community with others who practice Jesus. Jesus cannot be separated from His people, the church, His body here on earth. Practicing Jesus cannot be done alone. We are created to pursue Jesus, to follow Him, with others.

All other great religious leaders introduced a belief or philosophy. Confucius said, "Follow wisdom." Buddha said, "Follow the eight-fold path." Muhammad pointed to the five pillars of Islam. Only Jesus dared to point to Himself and say, "Follow Me." Any other religion, including the Christian "religion," is an idol if it replaces ultimate devotion to Jesus.

We have all been enslaved in some way to idols. But when Jesus captures our hearts and stirs our imaginations, we are set free from false gods—idols of our own making and idols thrust upon us by others—to follow Jesus. We are first transfixed, then transformed by Jesus. He fills the void at the center of our being. We don't need to imitate those who imitate Jesus, like a blurry photocopy of a photocopy. We can go straight to the source.

Jesus is duplicating Himself in the lives of thousands of believers, unleashing a movement of many "little Jesuses" who are given faith by His example and strength by His very person living in us. Jesus' life is our source of faith, and His example of service is our way to live; it is His person who lives through us.

Fear gets the best of many who want to follow Jesus. It robs us of our revolutionary fervor and turns us into weak-kneed trembling people. But Jesus will give us courage. He is our courage.

When Sally and I decided to move to South Africa, many friends and family members expressed alarm. "Doesn't South Africa have the highest crime rates in the world? Are you sure God is calling you there now? You guys should be thinking about retirement, not pioneering a new church and training center!"

The move to South Africa was not one we took lightly. We do live close to a community that has the highest murder rate in the world. One young man from that community told me that half of the women he knows have been raped. The initial response from whites here in South Africa was the same, if not more intense, than that of our friends back home: "Are you out of your mind? You could live in America, and you came here?" One young lady said to me, "Don't you know how dangerous it is here?"

We knew what it was like. We understood that it is a new nation, with many challenges. In fact, I have yet to meet a South African family that has not experienced a carjacking, rape, murder, or break-in. But I refuse to allow fear to motivate my decisions. Sally and I weighed the costs, considered all the practical issues, and made our decision in faith that God had a role for us to play in helping rebuild this wonderful country.

We believe this is Africa's hour. We believe that God has good plans for Africa, and that South Africa in particular has a major role to play in transforming the continent. The eyes of the world are on Africa: If God moves in transforming power here, a grassroots movement will be born that will capture the imagination and vision of people all over the planet. And we believe that is exactly what God is getting ready to do!

Jesus Did What? He Said What?

To provide you with some help as you seek to practice Jesus, I would like to point you to the first ten chapters of Luke as a source of inspiration. As you look at these practices and teachings of Jesus, the only thing that will hold you back from "practicing Jesus" will be a lack of imagination! Picture Jesus doing the things you read about, but in your skin, in your neighborhood. Think about Him doing these things through you, among pre-Christians. Get "church" out of your head, and put people who don't know Jesus into your head.

Jesus' teaching / practice	Implications for discipleship	How I can do it
The story of Jesus (Luke 1:1—4:18)	There is power in telling a story—your story is His story in your life	
Jesus listened and asked questions (2:42–52)	Spend time with others, asking good questions and listening	
Jesus gave special attention to the poor and marginalized (4:18–19)	Get involved with the disadvantaged	

Jesus selected and invited people to meet with Him—He "gathered" disciples (5:4, 11, 27–28)	Start a small group for pre-Christians	
Jesus gave His disciples freedom to create new expressions of church (5:36–39)	Do something intentional with non-Christians to build community	
Jesus practiced "see, touch, feel" (7:11–16)	Get your hands dirty serving someone in need—let it touch your heart	
Jesus allowed people to give to Him (8:3)	Allow the poor and marginalized to give to you and teach you	
Jesus healed people (9:11)	Pray for someone who doesn't know Jesus to be healed	
Jesus demonstrated and taught self-sacrifice and simplicity (9:23–26)	Give up a luxury or something you like for someone else	
Jesus practiced giving up power and authority over others (9:46–50)	Identify a way that you enjoy having power over others and surrender it	
Jesus took risks by sending His disciples out to preach and heal and stay in the homes of people they were reaching out to (10:4–6, 9:3–4)	Do the same thing! Find a person of peace and do what Jesus asked His disciples to do	
Jesus taught His disciples to help those beaten by thieves and taken advantage of (10:29–37)	Look for someone beat up by life or by thieves and lend a helping hand	

The Purpose of Practicing Jesus

What is the goal of practicing Jesus? Can there be any higher goal than becoming like Jesus—not in some ethereal, mystical way, but in a way of obedience that moves from our head, through our heart, and into our hands? But wait. Every sermon, every book, every sane Christian I have ever talked to, advocates becoming "like Jesus." What many have failed to say is that we are to be like Jesus *for the sake of others.* Heaven is our ultimate destination, but becoming like Jesus—how He lived on earth—is our goal here on earth.

We must not be guilty of so spiritualizing Jesus that we cannot relate to His life here on earth. If we deny His humanity, we will still praise Him but not model our lives on His earthly life. We will be comforted by a false spirituality that defines worshipping Jesus as singing songs and hymns but not living like Him in our everyday lives. By practicing Jesus we actually take Him off the crucifix, out of the worship songs, and make Him a real flesh-and-blood Jesus who lived here on earth and continues by living in us.

> Every sermon, every book, every sane Christian I have ever talked to, advocates becoming "like Jesus." What many have failed to say is that we are to be like Jesus *for the sake of others.*

Reflecting and Responding

1. Do a discovery Bible study on Luke 10:29–37.

2. Make a map of your immediate neighbors. Draw a diagram of the houses on all sides of you (up to nine houses), then see how many of their names you know and what you know about them.

3. Go over the list of teachings and practices from the life of Jesus listed in this chapter. Fill in the third column titled "How I can do it."

NINE

Sharing Jesus

Evangelism is not a ten-letter dirty word. Jesus is our example: He was not a wild-eyed fanatic standing on street corners, screaming at people, "Accept Me or else!" He preached to crowds and became friends with "sinners," but He did not use a "canned approach," pressuring each person into a "sinner's prayer." I can't find that approach in the teachings and example of Jesus. Whether it is four laws, five Scriptures, or any other "approach," sharing Jesus cannot be reduced to a method.

Despite our abhorrence of the abuses of evangelism, we must not define evangelism by our reaction to extremists. The desire to be *like Jesus* rather than *not* being like certain people should drive us back to the example and teachings of Jesus. He is our model.

What, then, is Jesus-style evangelism? To find the answer we must look afresh at His life and ask how Jesus related to people. For example, was Jesus a "silent witness," modeling but not meddling in people's lives? The favorite mantra of those who lean in this direction is, "Preach the gospel always, and if necessary, use words." But in my reading of the gospel accounts, that is not from the Jesus I read about. Can you really believe that, after reading how He interacted with dozens of people in the Gospels?

We can discover the answer to the question of what Jesus-style evangelism looks like when we consider how Jesus related to people. In my study of the Gospels I have found it very helpful to look at how Jesus related to three different groupings of people:

- Crowds: those that gathered spontaneously or at Jesus' instigation—they watched Jesus
- Seekers: those who responded to Jesus—some out of curiosity and some who were sincere
- Disciples: those who chose to follow Jesus—and whom Jesus invited to follow Him and learn from His way.

Let's go over these three areas of interaction with Jesus in a little more detail.

Crowds

These were people to whom Jesus reached out to intentionally, whether through preaching, healing or getting more deeply involved in their lives. On a broader level, the crowds were all those in Palestine to whom He had come to announce the arrival of the kingdom of God. He reached out to lots of people in order to influence as many people as could. He was just as intentional about reaching the crowds as He was individuals, but with distinctly different approaches.

Though Jesus wanted to reach as many people as possible, He spent far more time interacting with small groups and individuals than He did with large crowds, perhaps spending 75 percent of His time with His followers. Jesus saw interaction with the crowds as a way of planting seeds in people's hearts (Luke 8:4–18), a way of arousing spiritual interest, and a way of finding disciples to be taught. He was looking for those who were hungry for more, so He could invest His time wisely with them.

In every instance where Jesus interacted with large groups of people, He responded in one of seven ways:

1. He taught them and shared the good news with them.
2. He had compassion on them.
3. He healed scores of them.
4. He fed them.
5. He raised the dead.
6. He defended them from the religious leaders who abused them.
7. He inspired people to imagine life the way God intended.

The one thing Jesus consistently *did not do* in all His interactions with large groups of people was pressure them to become one of His disciples. He did not invite people to join Him as one of His close-up followers—He did that one-on-one. He did, however, try to arouse the spiritual interest of people in crowds, and He did speak to stir up their dreams and expectations for what could come from their lives if they sought after God. From a big-picture point of view, Jesus was aware and intentional about making sure that the people in certain regions knew about Him. He deliberately attempted to spread the good news of His kingdom to everyone in His sphere of influence (Matt. 9:35; Mark 1:38; Luke 13:22).

How do you apply the "crowd" idea to your life situation? Be aware that Jesus wants every person in your sphere of influence—all those in your relational and family network and in your immediate geographical setting—to hear the good news *through you.* You are not in these people's lives by accident. God has placed you there to share Jesus with them. There are a variety of ways to do that, including sharing your faith story, asking sincere questions to get to know people, listening and caring for them as friends, and following the promptings of the Holy Spirit as He leads you in responding to people's needs.

Reaching your "crowd" means praying for the people you are reaching out to. That does not mean you are personally responsible for each of them, but you will never fully know your part in taking Jesus to the people in your "crowd," including those at your place of work, university, neighborhood, village, and your city, if you are not praying for them to experience the love of God found in Jesus— through you. God has placed you where you are for a reason. You become the person God wants you to be by being a listening ear, someone to debrief with after a hard day, a safe person to talk to about the burdens of life. You influence people for Christ by visiting neighbors, walking around during coffee breaks at work, or taking time to hang out with fellow students in your school, college, or university.

Seekers

From the crowds came the seekers. In reading the Gospels we get the impression that there were people in and out of Jesus' life who were actively seeking to know more about Him. Some of them are made known to us in the gospel accounts, like Nicodemus, Zacchaeus, or the Roman centurion. They had listened to Jesus speak, seen Him perform miracles, or heard about Him and wanted to know more. Different people had different reasons for seeking Jesus: Some were sincere, others wanted to find fault with Him, and still others were motivated by curiosity. Some were desperate for help. Jesus' response to seekers was very different from His response to large crowds. He was more personal, but not always more "friendly." He was probing, questioning—and He almost always asked something costly from seekers. Jesus tested them, but in a proactive and loving kind of way. He would give them something to do, a step to take, to show they were prepared to pay the price necessary to actually follow Him. And Jesus did not continually dispense truth to seekers if they did not show that they were willing to obey what He had already taught them.

Jesus modeled for us how to arouse the interest of people through telling stories and doing miracles. But we also learn from Him how to ask seekers to go beyond spiritual curiosity or the miracle they have experienced—to hearing and obeying His teachings. If they took one step, Jesus led them to the next. Because we have the advantage of knowing the parable of the sower, we know that Jesus understood that the hearts of people were different. Some were hard, some were responsive; and of those that were responsive, not all were genuine or lasting. There are many examples of Jesus' interaction with this group of the not-yet-committed seekers as He invites them to be obedient disciples (Matt. 8:18–22; Luke 5:4, 27–28; 8:19–21; 14:26 (NLT); John 6:60–66).

If we ask people to pray to accept Jesus and then tell them they are Christians because they prayed the prayer, we are in danger of bypassing the crucial step of asking seekers to make costly choices necessary to be

His disciples. It is not something that can be done by merely praying a simple prayer. There are repentance decisions to be made. Jesus asks all those who sincerely seek Him to come with their whole hearts.

Jesus wanted everything. For Jesus, evangelism was disciple-making. He sowed the seed of love and good news to many people, then focused on those He discerned were sincere in their spiritual hunger, willing to pay a price to know the truth. He created a core group of disciples that He enlisted to go and tell others. What does this look like practically? I invite people to coffee, hear their story, then share my story the next time we get together. If there is interest to know more, we begin to meet regularly to study the teachings of Jesus through discovery Bible studies. I share more about how to do this in the last chapter of the book, "Start a Simple Church!"

Disciples

The disciples were those who had demonstrated their willingness to obey His teachings, not just listen to them. Understanding of what it meant to obey Jesus grew gradually in the hearts of the disciples as they put into practice the last thing He taught them. As they grew in their faith, Jesus selected some of His disciples for more responsibility. It says in Luke 6:13 that He chose twelve for more leadership responsibility.

At this point terminology can fail us. Many of Jesus' disciples were seemingly not fully with Him, yet they still wanted to be close to Him. Jesus deliberately left it that way. He did not draw up a list of rules like the Pharisees to decide who was "in" or "out" based on strict adherence to His "rules and regulations." He gave people room to wrestle with what they were hearing. Jesus desired their heartfelt obedience, but He asked for their obedience by drawing them to Himself rather than by establishing a closed religious society. But there was no question about whether He wanted obedience from His core team—that had to be absolute, because He stood at the center of the new community He was creating. There were people who were called disciples but who later turned away from Him (John 6:66). Jesus asked the Twelve if they too wanted to leave Him. Peter answered, "Lord, to whom shall we go? You have the words of eternal life" (v. 68 NKJV).

Apply This Practice of Jesus to Your Situation

Understanding the paradoxes of discipleship is crucial to this process of moving from crowds to a community of seekers to a core group of disciples. This is not a hard-and-fast method but a process to find people in whom we can invest our lives.

Sharing Jesus is partly about discerning the "crowd" in our lives, building relationships with a "community of seekers," and then selecting a core group of potential disciples to invest in. Sharing Jesus—what we typically refer to as evangelism—cannot be separated from a process of finding those who are truly responsive to Jesus.

Jesus taught how we can discern whether people are sincerely open to the good news (Luke 8:4–21). He respected people, but He also challenged them to go further in their search for God. In the parable of the sower, He compared the good news to seed sown into the soil of people's hearts. The soil represented four different types of people's readiness to hear His message. Jesus told this story to His disciples to help them discern the "soil condition" of people's hearts. In His parable, the sowers of the seed are the disciples themselves.

Announce. Preach. Proclaim. Teach. These New Testament words are often used to describe what Jesus did, what He trained His disciples to do, and what He told them to train their disciples and future generations of disciples to do, right down to us today (Matt. 28:18–20). "Presence without proclamation" is not what Jesus modeled and taught. The good news of Jesus is truth to be told: a message from God to be talked about, explained, and shared with those who will hear us.

Just as Jesus pictures the sower in the parable as one who generously scatters the seed on all kinds of soil, so we are to do the same. We are to share Jesus with all who will allow us, as long as we do that with both courage and decency. In the New Testament, the message is called the *gospel,* which literally means "good news." The good news is the life, death, and resurrection of Jesus Christ. It is the message we share with people that conveys the truth that God loves them.

A Person of Peace

In Luke 10, Jesus taught His disciples to look for people who were spiritually open and to stick with those people (vv. 5–7). They were to greet people they met in peace, and if they were welcomed, then that was where they were to focus their attention. I call that sort of person a "person of peace" because Jesus told His disciples to speak "peace" when they met such a man or woman.

Based on Luke 10, we can characterize a "person of peace" as someone who welcomes you into his or her life, who demonstrates spiritual hunger, who opens a network of relationships to the gospel, and who is prepared to obey Jesus. We find persons of peace throughout the New Testament: Peter brought his coworkers James and John to Jesus (Luke 5:1–10); the Ethiopian official went back to Ethiopia, where the earliest church in Africa was born (Acts 8:27); through Peter's witness, Cornelius and his household come to faith

(11:14); Lydia came to faith, followed by her family (16:14–15, 40); and the Philippian jailer came to faith along with his entire household (16:31–34).

How does the "person of peace" principle apply to us? Jesus wants us to find the people in our lives that God has been preparing for the good news. If we look for them, we can expect those who are people of peace to respond with openness. We should expect them, and look for them, and pray for them. They are in every neighborhood, business, residence hall, and university. They are your neighbors, your work associates, and your fellow students. The "person of peace" is the key person to have a transforming impact on a neighborhood, city, and nation. Those who are "insiders" will be more effective in reaching their friends and family than those of us who are "outsiders."

Belonging, Then Believing

People are often attracted to a Christian community before they believe the Christian message. I am not speaking about attending church meetings, but of being invited to be part of our lives through friendship and time spent together. When people actually see our love, they have a reason to believe in our loving Jesus.

Evangelism is not something you can stick into your schedule and leave behind when you go home. In fact, your home is the most effective place to do evangelism. That means you can't try to fit Jesus into

> You can't try to fit Jesus into your life; you must fit your life into Jesus. Evangelism and church are a lifestyle, not meetings to attend and duties to perform.

your life; you must fit your life into Jesus. Evangelism and church are a lifestyle, not meetings to attend and duties to perform.

Gospel Intentionality

I like the word *intentional.* It describes my journey of learning how to share Jesus with others. I find that I am most effective in sharing Jesus as I do ordinary things with people—but with intentionality.

That means I have to be ready to share Jesus with people. Seldom do opportunities fall into my lap. I prefer to prepare to be prepared—to be intentional. That includes being sensitive to people's needs, the struggles they experience, and the suffering of their crisis moments—and taking hold of these opportunities to listen, pray, and share with them. I do that by genuinely caring and listening to people's stories, praying for them, and then asking if I can share my story with them (if that has not already happened in the course of our conversation). The gospel is a message, and one of the most powerful ways to share that message is through the story of how I came to faith in Jesus. In chapter 1 of this book I shared my story of how Jesus became a living person to me. People with authentic, personal stories of coming to faith in Christ are never at a disadvantage to someone who disagrees with them—because it is their story.

Be ready to share your story. Get ready to be intentional (be intentional about being intentional!) by thinking about your story and writing it down. Practice by sharing it with a few friends. Ask them to give you feedback. Be able to tell your story of coming to faith in Jesus in a few minutes. Don't drag it out with lots of ugly details and boring tangents. Be interesting, and be honest. I believe that we often chicken out from sharing Jesus because we don't know what to say or how to say it.

Several years ago, while with a group of university students, I led the group in an exercise of writing down their personal faith stories and then had them practice sharing them with one another. A few were brave enough to share with the whole group. To be honest, I had a hard time smiling and looking positive while I listened. The stories that they shared publicly were quite boring, with no mention of Jesus, no reason given why there was a need for forgiveness of sins, and no emotion. They were about parents making them go to church, attending confirmation, and so on and so forth …

That experience made me a believer in the vital importance of intentionally *planning* how to share. As we tell our story, we should be intentional about including the major points of the gospel, the five parts of the God Story found in the prologue at the beginning of this book:

> **Creation**—God created us for relationship with Him; God loves us, and made us, and has a purpose for our lives. Tell how you came to believe this to be true and what difference it has made in your life.
>
> **Rebellion**—We have all, in one way or another, turned away from God. Rebellion against God can be an aggressive type of rebellion, or it can be a self-righteous, self-sufficient, religious kind of rebellion. In the story of the lost son, both the son who ran away from home and the older brother needed to experience the Father's love. Share how you came to realize that you had sinned against God.

Sacrifice—God's response to humankind's rebellion was to pronounce death and separation as our just punishment. But He didn't leave us there. He showed great mercy by taking our punishment through the substitutionary death of Jesus on the cross. How did you realize you needed God's forgiveness? This is an important part of every person's faith story.

Return—The fitting response to God's great mercy is to return to Him, acknowledging our sin and asking His forgiveness. What did repentance and returning to God look like in your faith story?

Commission—God first restores us to friendship with Himself, then He commissions us to share with others the good news of Jesus. And He has created us with certain passions, interests, and abilities, sending us out into the world to use those gifts purposefully to serve others.

When I share the God Story, I am creative and flexible. I look for ways to share these truths in ways that affirm God's love for people. I sometimes speak to people about how uniquely they are created, or about how the pain of the world we live in is caused by human selfishness. Write your story of how you came to faith in Jesus, then review it with others. Make sure your story faithfully tells who Jesus is and what He did for you in dying on the cross. Tell the God Story when you tell your story! Weave into your story these five truths of the gospel that I call the God Story. Remember, our story very naturally falls into three parts: our lives before we came to faith in Jesus, how we trusted Jesus, and what differences He has made in our lives.

Creating a Culture of Intentionality

You have the opportunity to create a culture of genuine gospel intentionality through your personal enthusiasm about sharing Jesus. You can encourage others to do the same when you gather in Bible studies, home groups, or youth meetings. Call attention to faith stories, including your own, in meeting times with others in your faith community. You naturally lead others when you inspire vision through the use of personal examples. Those who give the most hope, lead! If a leader has no authentic, personal story to tell, people will not take that leader seriously. Celebrate when people come to faith in Jesus or when they help others come to faith—that helps reinforce the culture of gospel intentionality. It also happens through public baptisms—an awesome time to celebrate the new life people find in Jesus. Some communities conduct regular commissioning times to send people into the workplace. Creating a culture of intentionality is something that grows when it is a natural part of the DNA of a community of believers. It flows vibrantly from the shared life of the community.

Tim Chester and Steve Timmis sum up this kind of intentionality:

> Above all we model the culture for one another so that it becomes the normal thing to do. The communities to which we introduce people must be communities in which "Godtalk" is normal. This means talking about what we are reading in the Bible, praying together whenever we share needs, delighting together in the gospel, and sharing our spiritual struggles, not only with Christians but

with unbelievers. We want our life together to be gospel saturated.[1]

Naturally, Organically, Relationally *Intentional*

We can be natural and intentional at the same time. We have decided in our All Nations community in Cape Town that we want our lives together to be gospel saturated, full of love and intentionality.

My wife, Sally, is wonderful at noticing people's names in shops and then going out of her way to love and encourage them. Like everybody else, we spend a lot of time waiting in lines in the shops we frequent. A while back Sally found herself the last in line at a shop. Some of those ahead of her were irritable and restless and complained loudly about the poor service. So, when Sally's turn came, she purposely reacted in a different manner.

She commented on how nice the salesperson was and asked her name. She found out it was Marie and asked her if that was her mother's name as well. Marie explained how her parents had known a wonderful Christian woman named Marie and that she had been named after her. Marie went on to tell Sally that she only attended church twice a year and had been wondering lately if that was "all there was to being a Christian"! They agreed to meet later to continue the conversation. At their next meeting, Marie confided that she had no idea why she had mentioned going to church but had been so impressed by the way in which Sally had acted toward her that she had just found herself pouring out her heart.

Another member of our community, Anna, has built intentionality into her life around art. She conducts art classes at the local school, offers art seminars, and, through them, builds relationships with young girls, discipling them through her passion for art.

Intentionality can be with the people we live with, but it can also be with strangers or those we barely know. Some time ago, I struck up a conversation with a lady across the aisle from me on an international flight into Johannesburg. We talked about the weather, how calm the flight was, and other things of that nature. As the conversation developed, she told me she worked for KLM Airlines and had been in Amsterdam for a training program. I asked about her work and how she enjoyed it, all the while praying silently that the Lord would lead in our conversation.

Eventually she asked me what I did for a living. I told her about our work with the poor. She gave me a surprised look, and I went on to tell her about how important my faith was to me.

She told me she was a Catholic and prayed to Mary. It seemed her way of saying, "You believe your way and I will believe mine." I noticed she watched me very intently to see what my reaction was. I didn't react and just said something innocuous about how important prayer is.

After some time, she looked over and asked me what I thought about praying to Mary. I thought for a moment and sensed the Holy Spirit's presence in my conversation at that moment. I said: "I have Catholic friends who pray to Mary because they don't feel they're worthy enough to pray to Jesus." I told her my story, how I had been set free from religious rules and regulations to enjoy a love relationship with Jesus, how it had suddenly hit me that I could be free from a *religious* relationship with God to enjoy a *personal* relationship with God through Jesus—because He loved me. "That is the most wonderful thing that ever happened to me," I told her. Big tears rolled down her cheeks. "I've never heard anything like that before. It's so beautiful," she said.

At that moment, the Holy Spirit was giving her an understanding of God's love for her. Our conversation carried on for some time. I didn't try to force something on her that she did not want, but I told her how she could have the same kind of relationship with Jesus. I had the satisfaction of knowing she left the plane with a clear and deep understanding of God's love for her and how she could respond to His love to make it her own.

Arousing Spiritual Interest

We may not always have the luxury to get to know people before sharing Jesus with them. There is a balance between the need to *earn the right* to speak about Christ and being *led* by the Holy Spirit to speak up. You don't always have to "earn the right." Jesus earned that right for us all by dying on the cross. On a long airplane flight, for example, there is only limited time to speak with others. In such a situation we must follow the Spirit's leading. Perhaps He wants us to jump right into the conversation and ask about a person's interests in spiritual matters. If a person's response is negative, that's okay; don't force the issue. We are to speak with courage but also with human decency. It is our responsibility to obey God—not to force a conversation.

Jesus was a master of starting spiritual conversations. He told stories with a point (parables) to arouse people's interest. They would think about what He had said and ask Him for more clarity. From there He would go on and share the deeper truths He wanted to communicate—if they were interested.

For example, John chronicled Jesus' conversation with a Samaritan
woman drawing water from a well. Jesus used the phrase *living water*
to get her attention, to arouse spiritual interest. It stirred the woman's
curiosity, and, by the end of their conversation, her life was touched
and changed forever (John 4:4–42). She was a person of peace—
she brought many others to listen to Jesus as well. Jesus spoke with
prophetic insight into the secrets of her life; He did this gently, not
to embarrass her, but as to stir her hunger for something more. She
responded, and, as a result, others responded as well.

Sharing truth plays an important part in evangelism, but ultimately the attitude behind what we say, rather than just the words
we use, makes the greatest impact. Genuineness and honesty, not
eloquence, will win the hearts of men and women. People want to
see that we really care for and understand them. Only then will
they open up to the message. It may take time, but it is time well
spent.

Some seem determined to bully others into agreeing with
them, regardless of the cost to relationships. They do not understand that we are called to be witnesses, not warriors. We are not
out to conquer those we speak to by sheer force of will and words.

I believe it is important to try to find common ground with the
person we're speaking to. It is much easier to work from some commonly held interest or belief than to start from scratch, with nothing
in common. It is not essential for sharing Jesus, but it is helpful.

Paul the apostle knew how to find common ground when sharing Jesus. He did it in the synagogues and in the marketplaces.
When addressing the philosophers at the Areopagus, Paul did not
say, "Listen, you misguided philosophers, you eggheads. Your god is

dead. You're wasting your time praying to idols. Be quiet, and I will tell you about the one true God, the God I worship."

Instead, he started out on common ground: "Men of Athens, I perceive that in all things you are very religious; for as I was passing through and considering the objects of your worship, I even found an altar with this inscription: TO THE UNKNOWN GOD. Therefore, the One whom you worship without knowing, Him I proclaim to you" (Acts 17:22–23 NKJV).

After finding a point they agreed upon, Paul went on to give a very clear summary of the gospel, adapted to their understanding. Some rejected his message, but others were won to faith in Jesus: "When they heard of the resurrection of the dead, some mocked, while others said, 'We will hear you again on this matter.' … Some men joined him and believed" (vv. 32, 34 NKJV). It is questionable whether any of them would have believed had Paul started by aggressively sharing the gospel and showing little regard for those in his audience.

You Aren't Qualified for the Holy Spirit's Job!

At times I have tried to be the Holy Spirit to others and have totally angered them and embarrassed myself. I have learned that, in His time and way, the Holy Spirit will convince people of truth. We must remember that it is our job to sow the seed of the good news in a person's heart and it is Holy Spirit's job to cause that seed to take root and bring a harvest of new life.

Jesus did not manipulate people. He did not try to back them into a corner where they could do nothing except what He wanted them to do. He always presented the truth and then allowed people the latitude to act upon it as they saw fit. We must be careful to follow Jesus' example in sharing the good news with others. Remember that, just as quickly as you manipulate people into accepting the gospel, someone else can manipulate them out of it. Far better for people to wait and be convinced of the rightness of the decision than to make a decision they are unsure of, without the indwelling presence of God to help them live it out. These people are not born again but stillborn.

In an instant world it's easy to look for instant results, but there are no shortcuts in sharing Jesus.

Patience *Now*!

In an instant world it's easy to look for instant results, but there are no shortcuts in sharing Jesus. There may be times when we spend weeks, months, even years praying for a person before we have the opportunity to share Jesus.

When Sally and I lived in Amsterdam, we had our hair cut at a small salon located in one of the city's tourist hotels. The owner was gay, and some of the customers were prostitutes. We wanted to form meaningful friendships with people outside our faith community.

Marijke, our hairstylist, was defensive when I sought to start a spiritual conversation. At times, I would pray all the way to the salon and while my hair was being cut, and still nothing happened. However, when I was tempted to give up I always heard the Lord saying, "Be patient. I'm going to touch her heart."

Then, after some years, a turning point came in an unusual way. A man who claimed to be a Christian came to the salon. He asked one of the girls out and afterward tried to seduce her. Everyone in the salon was indignant about the incident. What had upset them most was that the man said he was a Christian. The next time Sally went to the salon, Marijke told her the story and commented, "That man was not a Christian like Floyd. I trust Floyd. He would never do a thing like that."

Not long afterward I went to have my hair cut. I said to Marijke: "Thank you for what you said to Sally. I'm glad you trust me. Sally and I both love you and are very committed to you." There was a breakthrough that day in our friendship. We were able to be open and honest with each other in a new way, and many times when I went to the salon, she wanted to talk.

It took years of patience and perseverance with Marijke before the seeds of the good news began to take root in her heart. At times, it was frustrating and seemed pointless, but those years of perseverance, of walking across town to the hair salon while I prayed fervently, impacted her heart deeply.

Getting Started

Perhaps you want to know where to begin in sharing Jesus with others. If you are looking for some specific steps and help, let me suggest a few things to do:

1. *Pray regularly for three or four of your friends who are not followers of Jesus.* If you do not have such friends, it's time to start developing them. Ask God for ways to serve your friends. Ask Him how you can get more involved in their lives. Perhaps it will mean having them to your home or befriending them at work.

2. *Establish social relationships with the people you are praying for.* Invite them out for coffee. Listen to their stories. Build friendships with them through activities they enjoy. Develop mutual interests. Invite them for coffee again, and this time, share your story.

3. *Start spiritual conversations.* Ask them if they think about spiritual things. Ask them how they see God when they go through hard times. Don't preach at people or be the Bible-answer man or woman. Ask good questions, tell your story, and share God's Story. Be on the lookout for a person of peace, the one Jesus leads you to, who is hungry to grow spiritually.

4. *Invite people to whom you are reaching out to activities and events with friends who also follow Jesus.* We should be sensitive to what types of events they would be most comfortable attending. Remember, belonging is a step toward believing for many people.

5. *Invite them to do a Bible study with you for a few weeks.* If they continue to show interest, give the study a little structure and direction by using the ABC approach to your times together (see the last chapter). For a helpful list of topics and Scriptures to discuss, see appendix 1.

Overcoming Fear

When it is time to initiate a spiritual conversation, there is often a sinking feeling in the pit of our stomachs. We become worried about what the friend will think, and a feeling of insecurity and uncertainty grows. Thoughts flow quickly—*Will they reject me? Will they just think I am a fool?*

At one time or another, everyone has experienced fear when it comes to sharing Jesus with others. I know I have. Once when I was a young man, I went on a short-term outreach in Las Vegas, Nevada. We went from house to house, looking for opportunities to share Jesus. I went up to the first door and knocked. When the lady of the house answered, I said very nervously, "Hello, this is my friend John. My name is Jesus Christ, and we would like to talk to you about Floyd."

Fortunately, the humor of the moment broke the ice, and the lady asked us what we really wanted to talk about. I confessed my nervousness and then told her our purpose was simply to tell people about the joy and forgiveness we had found in Jesus. Much to my amazement, she stood in the doorway and listened for quite some time. She was deeply touched by the simple testimony we gave of our relationship with Christ.

Different Kinds of Fear

It might be helpful to examine more carefully the kinds of fear that can keep us from sharing our faith in Jesus:

The fear of rejection

We are raised from our earliest moments to look for approval from others, deeply afraid that people will reject us or think we are crazy if we say the wrong thing or act a little foolishly. People speak openly about their sexual exploits, political convictions, the weather, sports, and every other thing that enters their minds. Why is it that we, as followers of Jesus, do not want to speak about what is important to us? Obviously, we should not force the conversation in a certain direction. I find it helpful to ask people if I might share my thoughts with them about a certain topic or ask them a personal question about faith.

There comes a point when we must recognize that these inner fears we experience can produce sin if we allow them to get the better of us. If we allow our fears to determine our actions, then we have become a slave to our fears. The Bible says the primary way to deal with fear, as with all sin, is through confession (1 John 1:9).

The fear of losing our reputation

The best way to deal with this fear is to give up our reputation. We must be more concerned with what God thinks of us than what people think. The big question in life is not, "Can we trust God?" but "Can God trust us?"

> **The big question in life is not, "Can we trust God?" but "Can God trust us?"**

The fear of physical harm

I have experienced the fear of physical harm, walking through disadvantaged communities here in South Africa. I know what it is like to have threats against my life, so this is very personal and real to me. I have learned to overcome this fear by being honest with the Lord: "I don't want to die, but God, I will obey You. I feel that if I face a situation where my life is threatened, I might run away in fear, or worse, deny You. But Lord, I believe You are able to give me the grace I need when I face that kind of situation. I trust that You are able to help me in any situation I face."

Followers of Jesus in the early church also faced these kinds of fear. Look at the situation in chapter 4 in the book of Acts and how those disciples responded: "'They're at it again! Take care of their threats and give your servants fearless confidence in preaching your Message.... They were all filled with the Holy Spirit and continued to speak God's Word with fearless confidence" (vv. 29–31 MSG).

The best way to overcome the fear of physical harm is to acknowledge it; confess it as a sin if it is keeping you from loving people and obeying God; and then get involved. Ask God for strength to endure suffering for Jesus. He is able to give us the grace to face any situation in which we might find ourselves. But don't live in fear of anticipated danger to the point that you miss the joy of obeying God right now.

The fear of being inadequate

This fear makes us afraid that we will not have the right words to say when we talk to people, or that they will ask us a question that we will not be able to answer. This is the simplest kind of fear and the easiest to overcome.

If you lacked a particular skill for your work, you would most likely enroll in a training course. In other words, people take practical steps to get the tools they need to do the job they have to do. It is the same with sharing your faith. God can give us the tools we need to do the job.

In fact, as we gain experience, we begin to learn skills to share our faith. We can learn to anticipate people's questions, and we grow in confidence. What most people want to hear is your personal experience.

God is able to deliver us from all fears. In fact, the Bible says that "perfect love drives out fear" (1 John 4:18). One of the greatest ways to overcome fear is by praying for people on a regular basis and showing love to them in practical ways.

Reflecting and Responding

1. Do a discovery Bible study on Luke 9:1–4.

2. Reflect on who makes up the crowd, the community of seekers, and the core group of people you can disciple in your life. Ask God how you are to reach out to each of the three groups intentionally.

3. If you experience fear of evangelism, what kind of fear is it? Which kind of fear do you struggle with the most, and how do you deal with it so that it does not control your life?

4. If you have not done so already, write down your personal story of how you came to faith in Jesus. Practice speaking it out loud. Write it in three parts: your life before you trusted Jesus personally, how you came to faith in Jesus, and what differences Jesus has made in your life.

5. Review the five episodes of the God Story. Can you recite them now from memory? Discuss them with a friend or share them in your small group.

TEN

Suffering with Jesus

Some things take only a few words to say, like "I love you" or "I'm sorry," but no matter how sincere or true these words are, they lack meaning without time and action to authenticate them.

The same is true about the theme of this chapter. It takes little effort to say, "I will follow Jesus, no matter what," but there are difficult choices to be made if we follow Jesus in His suffering.

I don't want to waste words: If we follow Jesus, there will be suffering. I don't say that because I like suffering or believe we should all go out and "do some suffering." But Jesus' path in life led Him into suffering, so we must conclude that ours will as well—*if we follow Him on His path.*

Because of who Jesus is, and because the world is out of alignment with Jesus, it rejected Him, and at times it will reject us as well if we are known to walk the Jesus way.

Jesus endured the lack of understanding of His family, the betrayal of friends, the stigma of false accusation, misunderstanding and consequent rejection, the loss of rights, and ultimately, physical suffering and death. We probably won't endure any of these types of suffering if we don't rock the boat and just "act normal" as good churchgoers. By and large, institutional Christianity is part of the acceptable religious scenery in much of the world, tolerated as a "private matter" as long as we don't intrude on other people's lives. In fact, in many places it is to your advantage to be a religious person. But that is different from being a disciple of Jesus.

Jesus was everything but "safe" or predictable. He was wild and beyond human control. He was not a friend of institutional religion. He was a threat to political rulers as the leader of another kingdom (John 18:36). He disturbed the religious and powerful and comforted the broken and disenfranchised. He spoke against both the liberals and conservatives of His day when they oppressed or manipulated people.

> **Jesus was everything but "safe" or predictable. He was wild and beyond human control.... He disturbed the religious and powerful and comforted the broken and disenfranchised.**

When Jesus trained His disciples for service in His kingdom, He warned them that He was sending them as lambs among wolves. He told them there was a cost to following Him, and He asked them to count that cost. He warned them that He was sending them into the world and that some people in the world would hate them, just as they had hated Him. Jesus spoke very directly to this point, saying, "No servant is greater than his master," and, "If they persecuted me, they will persecute you also" (John 15:20).

After His first two and a half years of serving people through-out Galilee and Samaria, Jesus turned His attention to going to Jerusalem to face His appointment with death. Luke portrays the focused journey Jesus took to Jerusalem in chapters 9 to 19. It is in these chapters that He squarely faces what lies before Him and repeatedly cautions and prepares His disciples for the cross they must bear as well (9:57–62; 10:3; 12:8; 12:49–53; 14:25-32). Jesus faced dying on His cross and told the disciples they had to take up their cross if they intended to follow Him.

Dietrich Bonhoeffer said this about the cross in the life of a Jesus follower:

> The cross is not the terrible end to an otherwise God-fearing and happy life, but it meets us at the beginning of our communion with Christ. When Christ calls a man, He bids him come and die.[1]

The same invitation to "come and die" is given to us by Jesus today. The first disciples followed Jesus to His death; dare we think that following Him today means anything less to us? Paul the apostle didn't think so. He said, "For it has been granted to you on behalf of Christ not only to believe on him, but also to suffer for him" (Phil. 1:29).

Why Suffer If We Can Avoid It?

Personally, I have a healthy aversion to suffering. I prefer comfort and convenience and attempt to medicate headaches and bodily pain as much as my doctor will allow. I seek to avoid physical sacrifice if

I can. But I have also faced this truth: If I want my life to count, if I want to be true to Jesus, if I want to make a difference in the world, then I have to go against my natural tendency to avoid suffering. I don't believe in suffering for the sake of suffering, but I do believe in surrendering to the will of God if that means I can make a difference in people's lives. I believe in the beauty of human sacrifice and the ultimate good of suffering for the following reasons:

- The world needs brokenhearted people who have given their lives away. Most of the good that is done in this world for the poor and those who don't know Jesus involves risk and danger.
- Following Jesus means we go wherever obedience requires, no matter what the cost in sacrifice and suffering.
- Suffering is the privilege of every believer, especially those willing to follow Jesus among the poor, disadvantaged, rejected, diseased, and dying.
- Those who have never heard the good news of Jesus live in lands where the weather is extreme, the food is different, the languages are difficult, and the political environment is oppressive.
- Evil people, who rape and oppress and exploit, fight back if we dare to oppose them or stand up for their victims.
- Jesus Christ died for us, and His death prepares us to take risks, suffer pain, endure abuse, give up rights, and even die—without despair but with meaning.
- Suffering drives us closer to the heart of God more than almost anything else.

The Privilege of Suffering with Jesus

Our suffering is not so much *for* Jesus as *with* Him. He invites us to join Him among the lost, broken, diseased, abandoned, and hurting of our global community. Jesus is already there, beckoning us to join Him. He is there, offering redemption for people's lives, and because of their circumstances and the evil of this world, if we join Him we will probably suffer alongside Him. A sure sign that a person has given his or her life completely to Jesus is that person's willingness to suffer and make sacrifices with Him among the outcasts and broken of this planet. The whole point of being "crucified *with* Christ" is that we are liberated from self-rule, self-preservation, and self-promotion (Gal. 2:20; 6:17).

The sacrifice of Jesus enables us to leave father and mother and houses and lands for His sake and the gospel (Mark 10:29). It would be a great mistake to say that, since Christ died for me, I don't need to die for others, or that since He suffered for me, I don't need to suffer for Him.

> **A sure sign a person has given his or her life completely to Jesus is that person's willingness to suffer and make sacrifices with Him among the outcasts and broken of this planet.**

The reason Jesus died for us was so that we wouldn't have to die for our own sins, not so that we would not have to suffer or die for others. The call to suffer with Christ is not a call to bear our sins the way He bore them, but to love people the way Jesus loved them. Because Jesus died in my place, I do not need to cling any longer to comforts and conveniences. I can be content in His love and certain of His grace to enable me to make sacrifices that otherwise would make no sense.

Isn't this what Paul meant when He said, "I now rejoice in my sufferings for you" (Col. 1:24 NKJV)? Paul endured hardship and suffering to bring the good news of Jesus to people, and in doing so he suffered "with Jesus."

Jesus asked His disciples to "take up [your] cross … and follow me" (Luke 9:23). Clearly, Jesus expected that if they followed Him it would include sacrifice. We must not ignore or water down the call of Jesus to suffering and sacrifice.

Prepare to Suffer

To get good at something, one has to practice. My friend Michele Thompson works hard each year in preparation for the Argus Cycle Race. She cycles up and down the hills of the southern suburbs of Cape Town with dogged determination. She trains all year, but especially after the summer holidays in January and February. She not only wants to enter the race, she wants to complete it well.

The reason Jesus died for us was so that we wouldn't have to die for our own sins, not so that we would not have to suffer or die for others.

In the same way athletes prepare for their sports, we must prepare ourselves for suffering for Christ. How do we do that practically? In my experience, because I don't like suffering, and because I need all the help I can get, I do three things to prepare myself to suffer with Christ:

I *arm* myself with the truth.

   I *aim* myself in the right direction.

      I *act* in faith.

Let me expand on what these three mean.

1. Armed with truth

I arm myself with truth, especially this truth: Since Christ suffered in the flesh, it is a privilege for me to suffer in the flesh as well (1 Peter 4:1–12). I embrace it, meditate on it, and submit to it so I am not surprised when it happens, as if it is not my right or privilege.

I arm or strengthen myself with this truth by reading about or listening to stories of the lives of others who have suffered for Christ. I am inspired and strengthened by their examples when I see how God gave them grace to suffer, and the redemption He brought to others through their suffering.

One believer I have recently come in contact with who has "armed" me is David Watson. In his first nine years of a church-planting ministry, David planted twenty-four churches in some very difficult places, including seventeen among Muslims and Hindus in southeast Asia. In one country, David was arrested for preaching the gospel, spent eight weeks under house arrest, and then was kicked out.

Then David moved to India, where he began to work among the Bhojpuri, one of the largest ethnic groups and also possibly the people group most resistant to the gospel in all of Asia. David started learning the language and began to recruit and train people to take the gospel to this people group. In the first eighteen months of engaging the Bhojpuri, six men trained by David were martyred.

David was shattered by this loss. He left India and shut himself away for three months to, in his own words, "argue with God." He vowed not to return to India among a people where the cost was so great, unless God met him and showed him how to plant churches God's way. God spoke to David, enabling him to return to India. He prayed for five leaders to disciple and train, and David began to apply some basic discipleship truths that God had showed him:

- It's God's work to bring people to Jesus—our work is to find the ones He is preparing and to work with them.
- The Holy Spirit will teach the people He brings to Jesus—our part is to get them to the Word of God so the Holy Spirit can teach them in discovery Bible study.
- Everyone who listens and obeys learns from the Father— hearing is not learning, but obeying is. Our part is to be accountable in discipling relationships.
- Jesus works through counterintuitive discipleship paradoxes— our part is to learn the ways He works and to work His way.
- Obedience is a response to the presence and love of God— our part is to seek His presence and model that obedience out of love to others.
- Discipleship is about winning lost people, not training saved people—our part is to disciple those who don't know Jesus.
- Jesus trained people who trained more people—our part is to train trainers.

God gave David Watson five men and one woman to disciple, and David taught them the basic discipleship truths listed above.

These six people ranged from illiterate to very educated. There were no results in the first two years. In 1994 his mission board expressed disappointment with David because of the lack of fruit from his work. That year, eight churches were started.

Year by year more churches were planted. In 1995, 48 churches were started, followed by 148 churches in 1996. In 1997 and 1998, 327 and 526 churches were planted, respectively. And then, in 1999, over 1,000 churches were started.

These churches were not begun by "transfer growth" of other Christians. They were all new believers, converts from Hindu backgrounds. When David began working among the Bhojpuri people, a little more than ninety million people in number, there were about five hundred known Christians. Since 1994, eighty thousand churches have been started, and more than three million people have come to faith in Jesus.

In his early days of work among the Bhojpuri, when David sent in his annual reports, the mission board didn't believe the numbers. At the last pastors' conference David attended in India, fifteen thousand Bhojpuri leaders were present. And here is the most amazing fact of all: David did not start one of those eighty thousand churches. They were the fruit of David's discipling six people who in turn discipled others, who in turn discipled others … all in circumstances where there was great resistance to the gospel, and suffering and sacrifice were normal.

2. Aimed in the right direction

I "aim" myself in the right direction: where the poor and unchurched are found (Heb. 13:12–14). You may not be called to go to India or to work among the poor, but we are all called to lay down our lives for Jesus. That means "aiming" ourselves to where people don't know Jesus and where there is the greatest need. You must wrestle through with God where that is for you. It is vital for all of us to make ourselves available to gladly go wherever God sends us.

We have obeying Jesus inside out: we "plan to stay," and piously say, "I'm willing to go." It sounds spiritual, but it may be an excuse for making God responsible for what I should do—making Jesus known to as many people as I can, in any and every place He guides me.

Let's turn this slogan around and give it fresh meaning. Instead of saying, "I'm willing to go," while in our hearts, we're planning to stay, let's say to Jesus, "I'm planning to go, Lord ... show me where You want me to go, and I will go. I'll go across town, to my neighbors, or to any country in the world. Show me, and I will obey You, Jesus. I won't try to negotiate with You, Lord. I will take up my cross now and follow You."

3. Act in faith

I "act" in faith by getting involved where people don't know Jesus and where the need is greatest. We have to get involved with people to be able to act in faith. We can't be people of faith if there is no action. Faith without works is dead (James 2:17). Get involved with the poor; go on outreaches into Africa or other parts of the world; start a discovery Bible study group (see the last chapter for information about "D-Groups"); build relationships with your workmates, fellow students, and neighbors. Keep devoting your life to sharing the good news of Jesus with those who don't know Him (Matt. 28:18–20).

I prepare myself to "act in faith" by continually reminding myself of this: Where God guides me, He provides for me. When I face potential danger or weigh the risks of traveling to remote parts of the world to spread the good news, or when I simply count the costs of sharing Jesus with my neighbor, I strengthen myself with this truth: God's grace makes up for what I lack. When I face danger or potential suffering or risk rejection or misunderstanding at any level, I count on God to give me what I need in that moment. Otherwise, I know I will fail Him. So I choose to follow Jesus. I make the choice to trust God for all I need to obey Him, when I need it.

Reflecting and Responding

1. Reflect on Luke 14:25–28.

2. In this chapter, we discovered that it is a privilege to suffer for Jesus. How do you feel about this, and how do your feelings match the teachings of Jesus on discipleship?

3. What basic truths of discipleship did God show David Watson? Review and discuss them. Which ones can be applied to your discipling relationships?

4. What are the three ways of preparing for suffering with Jesus, and are you ready to do them?

5. Why is this chapter titled "Suffering with Jesus" instead of "Suffering for Jesus"?

Part Three

LOVING ONE ANOTHER

ELEVEN

A Committed Community

I want to tell you something not many church leaders will acknowledge, but most know to be true: Church is not a Sunday service, as in, "Which church do you attend?" It is not a congregation led by a "pastor," as in "Does your pastor preach good sermons?"

Jesus did not die on the cross to empower a hierarchical system of religious duties, with tithing and church attendance at the top of the list. Jesus came to unleash an irresistible revolution on the earth, not a predictable new religion.

Most churches are boring! They promote conformity, the exact opposite of what Jesus stood for. We are called to nonconformity. It is sad that church and conformity go together in most people's minds: Wear "decent" clothes, worship in a "respectful" manner, and believe "balanced" doctrine. Boring! When church takes the edge off being radical and the risk out of the adventure of following Jesus, church has died. It is no longer the irresistible revolution Jesus intended it to be.

This raises the question about the purpose of any form of church that does not call people to radical obedience. The Bible challenges the anemic idea people have of "fellowship," or "hanging out," or worse, being part of a weekly "home group" that has no vision beyond itself. If you are part of a small group, by whatever name you call it, and you are not committed to personal, radical nonconformity, transparency, and obedience to Jesus' commands to love the poor and the lost, you are playacting at church. The Bible presents church as familylike communities of people deeply committed to loving God passionately and loving one another with ruthless honesty—as they empower and encourage one another to live their lives for the poor and the broken. When we read Acts, we don't find people gathering in cozy home groups to merely "support one another," or just "hang out" as many postmoderns try to do. We find the disciples of Jesus in Acts sharing their lives and a revolutionary commitment to the cause of the gospel.

The first disciples did not just attend meetings that they tried to "juggle" or "fit" into their busy schedules; gospel intentionality was their life. They didn't try to "apply" the teaching of Jesus to their lives; His teaching was their life. Christian community was the very center of their lives because they knew it was the center of God's purposes on the earth.

I title this chapter "A Committed Community" because that is the choice we must make. We can love one another in a pleasant and comfortable

> **If you are part of a small group, by whatever name you call it, and you are not committed to personal, radical non-conformity, transparency, and obedience to Jesus' commands to love the poor and the lost, you are playacting at church.**

way and call that church, or we can love one another with life-altering commitment to obey Jesus together. If we are truly committed to community the way Jesus lived community with His disciples, it will take over our lives. We won't slink away and hide when people challenge us or call us to account for our choices. We welcome accountability because we know the world and the Devil are fiercely committed to sucking radical devotion to Jesus from the core of our being.

Cozy or Committed?

How you love Jesus determines what you believe about mission, and what you believe about mission determines how you do church. I used to think the three great loves flowed one into the other, like a cascading fountain: Our love for God fills us up and overflows into our love for one another, and that love then empowers us to love the lost. But that way of thinking sets us up for a false view of church and a safe "believers first" type view of what God expects of us. That paradigm leads to a "God wants me happy, healed, and safe, and then I can go out to that mean, harsh, dirty world and love someone" belief system.

How we see God's love for us sets the DNA for how we love the poor and the broken of our world. If our love for Jesus is deeply rooted in God's fierce passion to love us to the point of entering our messed-up, proud, and lost heart; if our love for Him is rooted in the fact that He loved us by giving up His rights and comfort to win us to Himself, away from our proud and stubborn rebellion against Him—then we will understand that to follow Jesus is to do the same for others that God did for us. What we experience and believe about God's passion to win the world back to Himself—this is what defines and determines our idea of church.

If we try to fit the gospel into our church lives, we will naturally want to have a relationship with other believers that is comfortable and nonchallenging, safe and loving. But if we believe the earth-invading incarnation is what gave birth to the church and is the reason the church exists, then we will long to journey with a committed community of like-hearted people. We will want a group of friends who do more than just smile and shake hands on a Sunday morning.

To make the choice clear, let me contrast the differences between what I term a "cozy" church and a "committed" church.

Cozy Church	Committed Church
Small group works when it's convenient	It's a new way to live
Safe people	Obedient people
Church is meetings to go to	Church is a community of allies
God's purpose fits around my life	My life fits around God's purposes
I fit what the Bible teaches into my life	I fit my life into what the Bible teaches
Make the gospel relevant to the world	Transform the world through the gospel
Mission is for missionaries	We're all called to obey God's mission
What kind of mission does God have?	What kind of mission does God have for me? What kind of me does God want for His mission?
Support group of close friends	Radical and loving friends who support obedience

God's Mission

Fully devoted followers of Jesus are not isolated individuals who do their own thing. Tim Chester and Steve Timmis say it this way:

FOLLOW

We are not saved individuals who then choose to join
the church as if it were some club or support group.[1]

When we come to faith in Jesus, we become part of the people who are sent by God into the world. This means that God's mission to save the world is our mission as well. I didn't say we are each sent as a "missionary" by God; God has one mission and one group of people to accomplish His mission: the church. The church exists to love and enjoy God by aligning our hearts with His great longing to bring glory to Himself in the whole earth. There are not "missionaries" and "nonmissionaries," but the obedient or the disobedient. When you came to faith in Christ you were mostly thinking about yourself, what this new faith meant to you. But then God began to reorient your life around Jesus and His commitment to love people through you. You became a "little Jesus" on His behalf.

Committed Church

I was reminded recently that the word *church* is mentioned only twice in the Gospels, and that's surely because church is not an end in itself. The first time church is mentioned is in Matthew 16, when Jesus asked Peter, "Who do people say the Son of Man is?" (v. 13). Peter answered correctly when he declared, "You are the Christ, the Son of the living God" (v. 16). Jesus started teaching Peter about church by asking about Himself. He asked Peter who he thought He was, because that is the focal point of church. Our view of church is determined by how we answer the question "Who is Jesus to me?" What we think of Jesus determines not only what we believe about Jesus but what we believe about church.

When I write about being a "committed" church I am not argu-
ing for being a more regular church attendee, but for shaping church
into a collective of friends who
share a passion for loving God, **Does God love us, and**
loving one another, and loving **is He concerned about**
those who don't know Jesus. **our safety and well-**
Being a committed member of **being? Absolutely. But**
a community means we belong **that does not mean**
to others who belong to Jesus, **our safety or comfort is**
and together we are committed **God's *greatest* concern.**
to loving people into being
Jesus' disciples. Being committed in this manner doesn't mean we are
perfect, but it means we want to learn to obey God. Loving one
another means we live out our love for one another by joining our
lives with other committed disciples in such a way that spreading the
gospel takes priority in our lives.

Cozy Christian Safe Theology

Cozy Christians have what I call a "safe" theology:

S—Self-protection

A—Avoidance of danger

F—Financial security

E—Escape from dangerous circumstances

Does God love us, and is He concerned about our safety and
well-being? Absolutely. But that does not mean our safety or comfort
is God's *greatest* concern. God's greatest concern is His glory—His
mercy being made known to people in need. God is glorified when
child sex-slaves are set free, child-headed households experience

help in their misery, drug addicts come to Jesus, workaholic fathers get their priorities right, families get healed and restored, and the unemployed find work. God cares about our safety, but He cares more about the pain in people's lives. Throughout history, God has received great glory through the sacrifice and suffering of His children as they followed the example of Jesus, often even laying down their lives for others.

Wild Lion or Tame House Cat?

Our view of church begins with this question, and how we answer it: "Who is Jesus to me?" For example, do we see Him as a nice house cat we keep around for comfort and companionship? Or is He like a wild lion no one can tame? Is He wild and beautiful, to be feared in your life? Or is Jesus sweet and cozy to you? If you see Him as wild and beautiful, to be respected and obeyed, then you will be prepared to adjust everything in your life around Him.

House cats can be ignored, but not lions. If a wild lion is in the house, you have to adjust your life around the lion. Jesus is a wild lion! If we see Jesus as a lion, then we will see church that way: not as a meeting to fit into our lives, but as a group of allies— like-minded coworkers—who are committed together to a cause greater than themselves.

In fact, we are not really living at all unless we are living for something or someone much larger than ourselves. The way to discover the destiny God wants us for is to invest our one and only life in passionate pursuits that dwarf our own self-interest.

Any discussion of church that doesn't begin with the real Jesus misses the mark. If we know who Jesus really is and appreciate what

He did in living His life among the poor and the lost, we will see church as an extension of His life. If we know who Jesus is, we'll do church the way Jesus lived. If not, we'll do church for ourselves, as an expression of our commitment to a safe, cozy lifestyle.

The Iron Gates of Hell

Jesus told Peter in Matthew 16:18 (NLT), "I will build my church, and all the powers of hell will not conquer it." The iron gates of hell are locking people in bondage. They are holding people captive in prisons of poverty, addiction, greed, and evil.

Remember the famous sculpture by Rodin called *The Thinker*? It depicts a man sitting with his elbow resting on his knee, his chin on his hand, thinking. My friend Neil Cole reminded me that it is part of a larger sculpture called *The Gates of Hell*. The Thinker is contemplating the gates of hell. Neil's aunt, who loves art, once startled him by commenting, "I could stare at *The Gates of Hell* forever."

Is this your experience of church—just staring at the gates of hell? Is this how you see the church, sitting and staring at people who don't know Jesus? Do you see the church running and hiding from crime and poverty and AIDS, busy maintaining programs to keep Christians busy and happy? Or do you see the church attacking the gates of hell to set lost people free?

Gates are not offensive weapons. We don't have to fear them. Jesus was telling Peter that hell is on the defensive, and through his faith and the faith of others like him, the church was going to break down the gates, invade the prison of hell, and set people free. Jesus was saying hell is on the defensive before the onslaught of the church. There is no force on earth that can keep the church from accomplishing the mission given to us by Jesus, the mission of breaking down the gates of hell—*no force … except our own lack of courage and obedience.*

If you see Jesus as one who has come to batter down the gates of hell, then that is how you will want to do church as well. Do you have a theology of going to people in need, even if there is risk to you? Or do you have a theology of being "safe"? Do you want to be cozy or committed? That is the question you must answer. Jesus commended Peter for his faith. Faith means taking risks. Faith means being on the offensive. Faith means you will have stories to tell of getting involved in the lives of the poor and the unchurched, of adventure and risk in the mission of Jesus. Not old stories, and not other people's stories. Your life is a story.

If you define church without the wild and dangerous hell-gate-attacking Jesus, you can "do church" without Jesus. But Jesus was committed to the point of coming to us, and He calls us to be committed to the point of going to others, to the point of being disciple-makers. Disciple-making is not something we do once people are converted; we make disciples by plundering hell and rescuing people from prison. We disciple the lost to be converted, not convert

We disciple the lost to be converted, not convert the lost to be discipled.

the lost to be discipled. Disciple-making is about being among those who don't know Jesus and finding ways to invite them on a journey with us toward Jesus. Church is a living, breathing, obedient community of disciple-makers. Jesus told Peter, "I will build my church." Will you let Him build it through you?

Will you commit yourself to join a few others and make disciples of people who don't know Jesus? Will you commit yourself to do that, no matter what the cost? Will you stir yourself to start making disciples right where you are, by praying and reaching out to your neighbors and family and fellow students and people at work?

In the remainder of the book, let's consider how we can join with a few others to be allies in the war we wage against evil and injustice and how God is working to set people free.

Reflecting and Responding

1. Do a discovery Bible study on Acts 4:32–35.

2. Take some time to reflect over the "safe" theology described in this chapter. Go back a few pages to remind yourself how we defined "safe." Are your beliefs built on being safe or on taking risks and being obedient to Jesus?

3. If you are willing to take risks to obey Jesus, write a prayer expressing your commitment. Tell Jesus what risks you are willing to take, and ask Him what risks He wants you to take.

4. This chapter states, "We disciple the lost to be converted, not convert the lost to be discipled." What do you think this means? Can you find an example of Jesus doing this?

5. In this chapter, we focused on starting with Jesus' question, "Who do you say I am?" as a way of determining how we define church and how we "do" church (Matt. 16:13–18). Why did you think Jesus started with Himself to define what church is?

TWELVE

Allies in a Global Awakening

Did you know that more people have come to faith in Jesus in the last sixty years than all the rest of church history in the previous two thousand years? A global awakening has reshaped Christianity into a truly world religion. For example:

- **Iran**—In the early 1970s there were close to three thousand known followers of Jesus in Iran. Today there are hundreds of thousands of believers—some say there may be as many as a million! That growth has taken place during a time of Islamic fervor and revolution.
- **South Korea**—In the year 1900, Christians were less than 1 percent of the population of South Korea. Today they are nearly 35 percent of the country. Seven of the world's ten largest congregations are found in its capital, Seoul. The world's largest Baptist, Presbyterian, Methodist, and Assemblies of God congregations are all there.
- **Nepal**—When I first visited Nepal in 1972 there were fewer

than 5,000 believers, and today there are more than 750,000 first-generation Christians in Nepal. Several years ago, the government was forced to change the constitution to grant freedom to follow Christ.

- **The Muslim world**—I believe the most incredible work of the Holy Spirit is happening in the so-called closed countries of the Middle East, North Africa, and Central Asia. Literally tens of millions of people in these regions of the world have come to faith in Christ. There has been suffering, and there are many issues of discipleship, but still—I cannot hold back rejoicing at how the Holy Spirit is drawing so many Muslims to Jesus.

- **Brazil, Cuba, and Latin America**—The explosion of new believers in Brazil almost defies imagination. And the stories of God's work in that country are repeated over and over again in other Latin lands: Argentina, Costa Rica, and Columbia. Perhaps the book-of-Acts story most hidden from our eyes in the West is the explosion of the church in Cuba. Under the harsh Castro regime the church has grown and flourished, led by simple servants of God who refuse to look to the West for money or models for how to grow spiritually strong church movements.

- **India**—The numbers are almost too much to take in, but one thing must be said: There is a vast movement of Dalits ("untouchables") that are migrating toward Christ in India today. Whole villages and castes and clans are tired of the abuses of Brahmin Hinduism, so they are seeking hope in Jesus. One medical doctor in North India told me he could not carry on his work because hundreds of people from one village were camping out in the parking lot of the hospital, refusing to leave until he baptized them. Wonderfully, the greatest breakthroughs are happening in north India in states too vast in size to comprehend.

- **China**—One respected journalist who has lived and worked in China for many years recently estimated that the number of believers in the underground church has swollen to over two hundred million.

Multiple Global Revivals

Like wild forces of nature, multiple revivals are happening simultaneously on our planet, out of human control. They have adjusted their features and ferocity in different times and places, but there is much for us to learn from them if we bother to hear the stories of the silent and unseen people who follow Jesus in these movements. These people are nameless and faceless to us, but they are known in heaven.

A Man Named Simon Zhao

One such leader is a man named Simon Zhao. Simon's life is gripping in its simplicity but convicting in powerful illustration of what it means to *follow*. Simon Zhao never appeared on television, didn't write any books, and did not seek fame or power. Yet his story is now being told around the world.

In the 1920s, a fledgling vision developed and eventually came to be called the "Back to Jerusalem Movement." God ignited a vision in the hearts of a small group of Chinese believers to commence a journey by foot from China all the way back to Jerusalem, sharing Jesus with those they met along the way. The vision formed into a mission to take the good news of Jesus to the regions of Asia that were dominated by the three world religions most resistant to the gospel: Hinduism, Buddhism, and Islam. Since the gospel came from Jerusalem to China, these believers felt it only right to return the favor.

In the 1940s, several small groups, compelled by a sense of urgency that the Lord's return was imminent, shared the vision to journey all the way to Jerusalem. One of the primary leaders at that time was Simon Zhao.

Simon burned with the vision. Joined by his new wife, Simon and his small team departed for the remote northwest area of China. Though times were troubled by civil unrest and travelers hazarded many perils from robbers, weather, and remote wilderness, they won many converts to Christ as they proceeded.

The team of roughly twenty-five members finally stopped in 1948 at Kashgar (also called Kashi), one of China's most westerly cities, to gather their strength and prepare to launch farther westward.

But just as they were about to step over the border, the iron fist of Communism descended on the land, and the borders clanged shut. Simon's group was still determined to follow the call to take the gospel west. When the Communists heard they wanted to cross the border, they decreed, "You're traitors!" and promptly arrested and tossed the Christians in prison.

Chinese prisons in the 1940s were basically death camps. Conditions in the coal-mine labor camps were horrific: a starvation diet; rancid food; grueling labor fourteen hours a day, seven days a week; sweltering summers and harsh winters; and daily torture. Healthy men could die in six months.

Simon's wife miscarried their first baby while in prison and later died herself. The other leaders also died. Simon Zhao had the harshest sentence, but he would not die. He realized God was preserving him supernaturally.

The months in prison turned into years. I cannot imagine the loneliness, boredom, hopelessness, and inhumane cruelty of Chinese prison life. On the verge of death at one point, Simon was transferred to another prison where he worked in a chemical factory. But being exposed daily to toxic gases and chemicals was hardly an improvement.

Nevertheless, Simon never let go of God. Nor did God let go of Simon. Simon prayed, "God, I cannot go to Jerusalem, but please raise up a generation of Chinese believers to complete the vision."

He was beaten, tortured, and abused daily, either by the guards or the other prisoners. But there were tokens of the Lord's grace in the midst of the hellish experience. On one occasion, the other prisoners locked him out of the barracks in the dead of winter, taunting him to see if his God would help him. Simon cried out to the Lord and suddenly felt warm all over. The prisoners were astounded to see steam rising off his body and the snow melting around his feet.

On another occasion, he was beaten so severely that his skull was fractured. While he was unconscious, the Lord came to him in a vision and said, "My child, I am with you ... I won't forsake you." Regaining consciousness, Simon touched the spot where his skull was smashed, and although there was dried blood there, the wound had been miraculously healed.

Twenty-five years became thirty, and thirty became thirty-five years in prison. All for obeying the vision the Lord had given to Simon and his band of faithful friends.

Simon had been given a forty-five-year sentence. After serving forty years, he was called one day in 1988 into the warden's office. He stepped gingerly before the warden, apprehensive that his sentence might be extended yet again for some unpredictable reason. To his surprise, the warden said, "The government of the People's Republic of China has decided to be merciful and lenient to you for the crime you have committed against our nation. I have been authorized to release you five years early. You are free to go."

Dazed, Simon shuffled out of the prison onto the streets of Kashgar. He was about seventy-two years old, his body carrying the marks of decades of beatings, torture, and harsh labor. China had seen so many changes that Simon could hardly recognize his own nation. He hadn't had a single visitor in forty years. Most of the people he had known were dead. Of those living, none had any idea of his whereabouts or that he was still alive. He didn't know his nation, and he didn't know a single soul. So now what?

He did the only thing he knew to do—he found a small room and prayed.

Eventually a believer stumbled onto him, and word leaked out among the followers of Jesus in Kashgar: "A brother is here who has just survived forty years in prison for his faith." When the news made its way to eastern China, the believers were stunned. Forty years in Chinese prison? Unthinkable!

In 1988 the revival among the underground churches in eastern China was perhaps at its zenith. New converts were coming to Christ daily in droves. And nowhere were the flames hotter than in Henan province. Dubbed by some the "Galilee" of the movement, Henan was the epicenter of the underground house church in 1988.

Some of the believers in Henan learned of Simon's existence and immediately sent a delegation to Kashgar with instructions to bring Simon back at all costs. When they found him, they eagerly asked him about his experiences. He simply and meekly said, "I served forty years in the Chinese penal system." They asked him to return to Henan with them, but he politely declined. They responded with persistence, "But you must come back with us. You have an important story to tell, and the church needs to hear your story."

He would not be easily persuaded. His visitors entreated him, "But you don't understand. While you've been in prison, God has ignited a powerful revival in China. We have hundreds of thousands of young people pouring into the kingdom who need to hear your story. They need to catch the vision of going back to Jerusalem to preach the gospel. God will use you to ignite within them a passion for China's role in the global harvest. All you need to do is simply tell your story. We need you—you must come!"

"God told me to go west, not return eastward," he announced.

But when Simon saw the determination of the delegation, he realized he had little choice but to honor their wishes. The Lord confirmed to him that it was the right decision, so he returned with them to Henan. They didn't have enough money to buy him even a reserved seat on the train, so he curled up on a newspaper on the floor as he made the journey eastward with his four traveling companions.

When he arrived, he was greeted like a war hero. Instantly in demand, he began to travel among the house churches, imparting the vision for global evangelization by the sheer force of his personal story and the power of the Spirit's anointing.

God allowed the vision He had placed in Simon's heart to be crushed. We don't know why God allows such suffering, except that it is the way of cross, and if it was worth His suffering and dying, it is worth our lives to follow His example. God brought Simon through suffering and multiplied his efforts in the lives of the young men and women who were inspired to evangelize Muslims, Buddhists, and Hindus on the road back to Jerusalem.

Worthy Is the Lamb!

There is an ancient rallying cry of the church, passed down through the centuries, beginning with John the beloved disciple. It was John who wrote, "Worthy is the Lamb ... to receive ... honor and glory and praise!" (Rev. 5:12).

Worthy is the Lamb! The Moravians and many others down through the centuries took up the rallying cry: "Worthy is the Lamb to receive the reward of His suffering!"

God allowed Simon Zhao the privilege of suffering with Jesus. Only heaven will reveal his reward for such faithfulness to the Lamb. God allowed the vision He placed in Simon to be totally crushed. He allowed the adversary to batter Simon's physical body and spirit. But God's grace preserved his life, and his spirit was not broken beyond what Simon could bear. And then God allowed the vision to be resurrected, and Simon's life was multiplied many times over. Instead of Simon touching a few remote villages, a flame was lit in the hearts of thousands of fervent believers, and the impact was felt by many.

Simon Zhao died on December 7, 2001, but not before God had given him thirteen years of fruitful ministry among the Chinese underground church. Many caught the vision and took up the call to go west to reach Muslims, Hindus, and Buddhists with the good news of Jesus. God used Simon's extraordinary life, like a grain of wheat, a seed, to fall into the ground and die, and a thousand times over it was raised from the ground. The seed that is Simon Zhao's life produced much fruit for the kingdom of God.

Allies with Simon Zhao and the Underground Church in China

If you follow Jesus with your whole heart, you are an ally of Simon Zhao and other brothers and sisters in China. Simon's life is a reminder that, as followers of Jesus, God will give us the grace to live our story right where we are. If we live our story, we will inherit in the life to come multiplied blessings, including the smile of Jesus when He says, "Well done."

Maybe you don't believe that you qualify to be part of a global awakening? Do you feel your faith is too weak? Don't really care about a "global" awakening? If so, I want to remind you of Jesus' words to the first disciples when they were in a similar frame of mind:

> Anyone who believes in me will do the same works
> I have done, and even greater works … You can ask
> for anything in my name, and I will do it, because
> the work of the Son brings glory to the Father….
> I will ask the Father, and he will give you another
> Counsellor, who will never leave you. He is the

> Holy Spirit, who leads into all truth. The world at
> large cannot receive him, because it isn't looking for
> him and doesn't recognize him. But you do, because
> he lives with you now and later will be in you.... I
> will not abandon you. (John 14:12–13, 16–18 NLT)

These words contain the essence of the challenge we face: What do we ask for? What do we want deeply, intensely, passionately? The disciples of Jesus were concerned about the issues of life, such as children and family and jobs and their future. They lived in a nation that was occupied by a foreign power. They were under the rule of ungodly dictators.

But Jesus wouldn't let them off the hook because of the pressing cares of life. He beckoned them to live for eternity, not to be captured by the anxieties of life. Jesus desires to be the source and goal of all we do. So we are invited to do what we do in life because of Jesus (our source) and for Jesus (our goal). He gives us all we need to obey Him. Relying on the comforting words Jesus spoke to them, the first disciples set out on a lifetime journey of obedience and discovery. They learned, they made mistakes, and they grew—because they obeyed the words of Jesus and because they did it together as allies in the same struggle. If you will continue on that same journey, you will grow spiritually more than you ever dreamed possible.

Don't Go It Alone

You won't make it on your own. If you are isolated, you are in danger. God created us to be part of a committed community, a local spiritual family dedicated to obeying the Great Commission and the

Great Commandment. If you can't find others who believe as you do, find a few people who don't know Jesus yet, and ask them to do it with you. Be honest and tell them you want to learn how to understand and obey Jesus, and see if they want to learn to follow Jesus with you. Does that sound a little extreme? It's how Jesus did it—He called people to *follow*, and His disciples did exactly the same thing.

Remember, you are part of something started by Jesus. This is not my idea or yours. Jesus started us on this journey, and Jesus will complete what He began.

Movements

I have dreamed of being part of global movements to Christ since I was a student in university. I have helped start some small movements to Jesus, and though I'm older now, I dream of catalyzing massive discipleship movements in Africa and the Muslim world. That is why I moved to South Africa. When I visited this country before we moved here in 2006, I saw the stirrings that I was convinced would touch all of Africa—even beyond Africa. Sally and I are permanent residents in South Africa now because we believe it is going to happen here. In fact, it has already begun. Men's conferences called "Mighty Men" have filled stadiums and attracted more than two hundred thousand men to receive marching instructions in the movement. The "Global Day of Prayer" is providing prayer fuel for the movement through powerful intercession. Student churches on university campuses fill with young men and women with a contagious eagerness for sacrificial service.

I have taken some of the things I have learned about movements, and some of the things described by my friend Steve Addison in his book *Movements That Change the World*, and integrated them in the six benchmarks below. I share these benchmarks to let you know what you are part of and to inspire you to expect more.

Six Benchmarks of a Movement

1. Passionate faith

Movements of Jesus followers are unleashed by the presence and power of God as ordinary people are led by the Holy Spirit, faithfully obeying the Word of God and actively sharing Jesus with others. As we have already observed, faith does not mean the absence of fear, but obedience in the face of fear. Such faith is contagious. Spirit-led followers of Jesus cannot help but infect others when they exercise such faith.

2. Commitment to a cause

Followers of Jesus change the world when they share a common vision that is in alignment with deeply held beliefs. This enables them to build a culture with other followers that sustains and reinforces their passion. Their vision will bring them into conflict with the world around them, but if they continue to connect with the world, they will help change it. Followers of Jesus are distinct from the world but are, at the same time, engaged in the world. Steve Addison points out that it is the combination of these two elements of connection and distinction that causes a movement to be a catalyst for transformation.[1]

> **Followers of Jesus are distinct from the world but are, at the same time, engaged in the world.**

3. Contagious relationships

Being close to people of faith who speak openly of their love for Jesus is what leads other people to faith. Committed communities turn into movements and grow exponentially when the gospel spreads along existing lines of relationships. When we "Christianize" people and, by our example, teach them that they don't have to speak up about Jesus, we cut them off from their relational networks and marginalize them from their culture. For a movement to continue to grow, people must continually reach out to their own culture and social networks.

One of the most "contagious" people I have met in South Africa is Mandi Hart. Mandi loves people, and though she is a woman of deep faith, she refuses to be cut off from friends who see things from a different perspective. Mandi continually reaches out to build relationships with neighbors, other mothers, business associates, and those who are going through a hard time. Mandi makes you believe you can do the same thing by her lifestyle and her enthusiasm for people. She is a busy mother of two growing children, married to a businessman, and loves horses, kids, and life. In other words, she is "normal." But she actively seeks to share Jesus in wise and loving ways, and because of that she has helped many others come to faith in Jesus.

4. Rapid mobilization of ordinary people

Church buildings and paid church leaders are the greatest hindrance to the growth of a movement. If paid leaders are not careful, they model a form of leadership that is not easily and rapidly transferable. The rapid spread of a movement happens through the efforts of nonprofessionals and of those who are not dependent on funding for "the ministry." Grassroots visionary leaders in a rapidly growing movement should inspire a common vision, model the core beliefs, assist those they recruit by coaching and mentoring, evaluate and give feedback, then get out of the way so others can get on with the job. Cautious or controlling visionary leaders will drive away future visionaries and stifle momentum in a movement.

5. Adaptive methodology

To accomplish their mission, followers of Jesus who long to see a movement of disciples making disciples are prepared to change everything about themselves except their core beliefs. Movements adapt and change everything to be more effective: the way they do church, programs, and structures. They contextualize

Cautious or controlling visionary leaders will drive away future visionaries and stifle momentum in a movement.

church, but they don't try to contextualize the gospel. They understand the difference between the wine skins and the wine (Luke 5:36–39), i.e., between the gospel and the cultural packaging of the gospel. They don't get married to the form or packaging but are in love with the gospel itself. To quote Steve Addison, "Movements pursue their mission with methods that are effective, flexible, and reproducible."[2] The goal of a movement is to find forms and models that are easily transferable, so that the movement surpasses the first generation of leaders.

6. Multiple generations of disciples

Movements multiply through enlisting multiple generations of disciples. Movements gain unstoppable momentum by passing on their core beliefs from one generation to another, again and again, through making disciples. If we follow the practice of the apostle Paul, we will train each generation of disciples to multiply themselves by at least four generations, and in this way multiplication will be built into the makeup of the movement. Paul said to Timothy that he should train faithful followers of Jesus who would train others also. Four generations of disciples are represented in these verses: Paul, Timothy, Timothy's disciples, and those discipled by Timothy's disciples (2 Tim. 2:2). If we consider Barnabas, who discipled Paul, there are five generations of disciples. Barnabas, Paul, Timothy, and their spiritual sons and daughters were part of a multigenerational movement to Christ. It had unstoppable momentum.

Movements gain unstoppable momentum by passing on their core beliefs from one generation to another, again and again.

Multigenerational Movements

Many multigenerational movements of Jesus followers are happening in our world today, most of them found in Asia, Africa, and Latin America. By multigenerational I don't mean children, youth, and parents all finding a part in the church, but one generation of believers raising up the next generation—having spiritual sons and daughters. One movement in China that started in the late 1990s now has over six million adherents! At last count there were twenty-six generations of new believers, with a 90 to 95 percent adherence to first-generation biblical truths. These movements are made up of people who work long hours in factories and farms, who sacrifice their time and energy to make Christ known. Why such phenomenal growth? Because faithful men and women have passed on what they received, and their disciples did the same thing, often at great cost and sacrifice. (In the following two chapters I will share how we are applying the lessons we have learned from around the world in the movement I am part of and how you can ignite a movement as well.)

One young follower of Jesus told me a few years ago that his dream was to start a movement of eight spiritual generations of believers because he was the eighth-generation believer of his pastor. He then named each person, one after another, who had led someone to faith in Jesus, who in turn led someone else, and finally he named the person who had led him to faith in Jesus.

I have pledged my life to be part of what God is doing in the earth. Not what church culture is doing, not every little whiff of doctrine that blows through town, but what God is doing to bring the lost to Himself and to transform the way people live. As long as God gives me strength, I will follow Him, I will train others to follow Him, and I will empower them to make disciples "who teach others also." I invite you to join me. A global awakening is taking place, and I for one don't want to miss it!

Reflecting and Responding

1. Jesus desires to see movements of disciple-making disciples fill the earth, and we have to count the cost of following Him if

we are to be part of such a movement. Read Luke 6:46–49 and then do a discovery Bible study on this passage.

2. In this chapter, we spoke about being allies in a worldwide movement started by Jesus. What does the word *allies* mean, and what does that imply for your involvement?

3. Who are potential people that you can disciple to faith in Jesus who could possibly disciple others also? Make a list of them and pray for them.

4. Reflect on the six benchmarks of a movement and turn them into prayer points for yourself and for those you disciple. Which characteristic is most challenging to you, and why?

THIRTEEN

Gut-Level Transparency

Being allies with other followers of Jesus won't happen without gut-level transparency and accountability. Living a lie happens when we hide our lives from one another and create a breach in the alliance we have. If we don't really know the people who follow Christ with us, we can't really love one another, and we certainly can't go into spiritual battle together.

John wrote in the New Testament, "If we walk in the light as He is in the light, we have fellowship with one another, and the blood of Jesus Christ His Son cleanses us from all sin" (1 John 1:7 NKJV). Some Christians throw the phrase "walking in the light" around quite a bit. The phrase adorns posters, napkin holders, and T-shirts. Yet despite its usage in popular Christian culture, I wonder if many of us know what it really means to "walk in the light."

The phrase *walking in the light* has a very spiritual sound to it, but it has a very down-to-earth application. It means living in a state of gut-level honesty, with the thoughts of our hearts and the secret behaviors of our lives known to both God and those to whom we are accountable.

Loving God, loving the world, and loving one another are dependent on the power of genuine love. How can we love God if we keep Him out of our lives or hide things from Him? Transparency is a willingness to be known as we really are, to be open about our lives, with both God and others. Being transparent means voluntarily being open and frank about what is happening in your life—without distorting the truth. It means taking the mask off and letting other people see the real us.

Being Real with God

When God called us to work with street people in Amsterdam's red light district, pornography was rampant, and prostitutes sat in picture windows trying to lure customers. As I walked up and down those streets day after day, I found the only way to keep my thoughts pure and clean was continually to remind myself that I was in God's presence. I was not just an inquisitive tourist peering into windows or trying to catch a glimpse of what lay behind the well-guarded brothel doors.

If an unclean thought came into my mind, I learned there were three things I could do to be "in the light." First, I could be honest with myself. If an impure or unclean thought came into my mind, I needed to acknowledge to myself that it was impure and then make a choice to turn my mind to something wholesome. Second, I could bring the thought to Jesus. The act of bringing and telling the thought to God in prayer is one of the ways we "walk in the light."

And the third thing I could do to walk in the light—and it was a tangible expression that I was serious about being a transparent person—was that I would confess my sins and temptations to a few fellow believers. I did that regularly. We formed small groups of a few men or women—not mixed—for transparency and accountability. We knew we were in a war zone and that we could not make it on our own.

There is power in the light. There are no pockets of darkness in a well-lit room. Darkness only exists if an object blocks out the light and throws a shadow. Refusing to confess our sins is one way in which we cast shadows in our spiritual lives. If we are not careful to remove those shadows by acknowledging our sins to ourselves, to God, and to a few others, we will have darkness in our lives. Though I have mentioned sexual issues, "darkness" can include thoughts of resentment, jealousy, criticism, and anger.

When I confess my sins to the men who have agreed to walk together with me in accountability, they don't respond with: "You did what? We're shocked! That's the worst sin we've ever heard of!" Ecclesiastes tells us there is nothing new under the sun, and nothing could be truer. Read the Old and New Testaments, and you will find every sort of sin and failure. But read too of the God who forgives, who picks us up and puts us on our feet once more on solid ground.

Confess Your Sins

Find another Christian who, as far as you know, doesn't have the same problem you have, and open up to him or her. Preferably do that in a group of men or women you meet regularly with, so that you really do know one another. Be prepared to do that with believers and nonbelievers in the same group. Why do that with nonbelievers? Because it is a way to be an example of honesty and accountability.

At times like these, you may think, "I can't tell anybody what I've done—it's too bad!" or, "No one will ever talk to me again if he or she knows what I'm really like." But these excuses will keep us from forgiveness and the victory available to us by walking in the light.

There is a false teaching that says, "Your sins are under the blood of Jesus, so nobody else needs to know about them." This is a half-truth, which fails to acknowledge our need to confess our sins to one another (James 5:16). Telling other Christians about our sins does not provide for our forgiveness; only the death of Jesus on the cross is sufficient to forgive us our sins.

> **There is a false teaching that says, "Your sins are under the blood of Jesus, so nobody else needs to know about them."**

Confessing our sins to others allows us to walk in freedom, making it all the more difficult for sin and the Devil to get the upper hand over us. It also assures us of God's love when others know us completely and still accept us.

Think of all we would have missed if the Bible recorded only the triumphs of its main characters. Because we know of David's sin with Bathsheba, the beauty and grace in Psalm 51 minister to us so much more effectively in times when we need forgiveness. Likewise, many of us like to read about Peter because we find ourselves mirrored in his personal struggles. We identify with him. And Jesus Himself struggled with His emotions, and eventually in the garden of Gethsemane He won the victory over them. We know about Jesus' temptation not to suffer on the cross—because He shared with the men who were close to Him, and they in turn told the story in the Gospels so we could be strengthened by His example (Matt. 26:36–46).

It is not a sin to be weak! But it is foolish to be weak alone when, through the commitment of other brothers or sisters, God has provided us with His love for our support. Christian maturity means coming to a place of acknowledging our weaknesses as an opportunity for growth. Paul clearly grasped this point when he wrote of God's promise to him: "'My gracious favor is all you need. My power works best in your weakness.' I am free to tell others about my weaknesses, so that Jesus can accomplish His work in and through me." (2 Cor. 12:9, author's paraphrase).

There is a tendency for those who have been following Jesus for some time, or who hold positions of spiritual leadership, to convey the impression that they are beyond temptation. This is dangerous, both for those who think it and for others who may believe them. We all need to go on record saying that we believe in transparency and accountability and that we practice it in a discipleship group. All of us, regardless of our years or position, face temptation and struggle in our lives. There is potential for sin in the heart of every person, and only by taking it seriously and being accountable to others with whom we are journeying with Jesus, can we have victory over sin.

There are many Christians faking it. They are acting happy and spiritual on the outside, but on the inside they struggle like the rest of us. They have not learned the freedom there is in being transparent. It is time for all of us to take off our masks and begin experiencing the joy that comes from walking in the light with godly humility.

> There are many Christians faking it. They are acting happy and spiritual on the outside, but on the inside they struggle like the rest of us.

My Secret Sin

Paul tells us in Romans 13:13–14 (NLT),

> We should be decent and true in everything we do,
> so that everyone can approve of our behaviour. Don't
> participate in wild parties and getting drunk, or in
> adultery and immoral living, or in fighting and jeal-
> ousy. But let the Lord Jesus Christ take control of
> you, and don't think of ways to indulge evil desires.

Don't think of ways to indulge evil desires. To put it another way, this means we are not to put ourselves in a place of temptation, either to prove how strong we are or because we are denying that we have a weakness in a particular area of our lives. Followers of Jesus must flee temptation, not flirt with it.

Okay, it's time for me to walk in the light. I love ice cream—ice-cream sundaes, ice-cream cakes, ice-cream cones, and ice cream right out of the carton! Now, to impress my wife with my self-control, I could ask her to make homemade double-chocolate ice cream with walnuts and almonds. Let's say I ask her to leave several scoops of it in bowls around the house: one beside my bed so I can see it when I go to sleep, another in the bathroom to tantalize me while I shave in the morning—all because I want to impress my wife by resisting temptation at every turn!

Such a scheme would be a disaster! If I don't want to eat ice cream, then why torture myself by having it constantly before me? If I am proving anything at all, it is how foolish I am. Alcoholics Anonymous does not encourage those trying to break free of the bondage of alcohol to sit night after night in a bar to prove that they have overcome their problem. Areas of weakness in our lives are difficult enough to overcome without added exposure to temptation.

If you want to be serious about overcoming temptation, take the steps necessary to avoid sin. Focus on pleasing Jesus. See it as a way of saying yes to living a holy life, not as a way of saying no to sin. It is much easier to say yes to Jesus than to say no to the temptations we face.

If your weakness lies in getting too physically involved when alone with someone on a date, then why continue being alone time after time? All too often we wait until sin is right within our reach before seeing whether we have the self-control to avoid it.

The Bible says, "If you think you are standing strong, be careful, for you, too, may fall into the same sin" (1 Cor. 10:12 NLT). It's true. We are all capable of being tempted and falling, and failure to admit it means we are not properly guarding ourselves. If we have a weakness, we should not put ourselves in a position where we will be tempted to give in to it. If I don't want ice cream, I should not order it and then have to sit staring at it. If I don't want to spend my time slandering others, then I should not develop close relationships with those who make a habit of criticizing and gossiping about others.

How Sin Patterns Get Entrenched

Some people become very concerned when, after renouncing their sin and walking in the victory Jesus brings, they find that they still feel vulnerable to the sins that formerly had power over them. I think of this like the dry riverbeds I come across in the bush. A rutted riverbed is often dry for years at a time. When the rain comes, the water rushes into the riverbed and flows along, easily following the course of dry, well-worn ruts formed in the past.

Our minds are like those riverbeds. We get into the habit of thinking and reacting in certain ways, and when the temptation arises, we easily fall into the old ways. There is an old proverbial saying that goes like this:

> Make a thought, reap a choice;
> Make a choice, reap a habit;
> Make a habit, reap a character;
> Make a character, reap a destiny.

When we totally give our lives to Christ, we are given power to overcome sin. But the old, dry riverbeds of habits and thought patterns are still there. The power that once held us in those habitual ruts has been broken, but the ruts are still there. Those old sin patterns are the ones most likely to trip us up and are the easiest to fall back into. The good news, however, is that Christ has freed us from the power those patterns once exerted over us. As we grow in Christ, those old ruts will also be washed away. But it usually takes time, and in the meantime we have to be alert to the old ways and beware that we do not fall into them again.

The Rules Are the Same for Everyone

The same truths of transparency and accountability apply equally to all of us, no matter what position we hold. Whether you are a business leader, an official in the government, a leader in the church, or a typist in an office, the same basic truths of discipleship apply to all of us. Transparency is one of those basic truths that apply to all who seek to follow Jesus. It is tempting to cover up sin, to override accountability and put oneself above the need to be open and honest. But to do so is to set oneself up for a big fall. Sooner or later our hidden sin will be exposed. Either we can be transparent out of our love for truth, or God will deal with it out of His love for us.

We are not in this alone. We have brothers and sisters to go with us on our journey with Jesus. Faith communities all over the world are learning the power of living transparent lives together. Recovery groups and support groups are tapping into the power of not going it alone. I call these groups D-Groups, or "discovery groups." We named them after a simple Bible-study method taught by David Watson. The name is not important, but the power of being transparent and accountable is. Let's learn more about how to do that in the final chapter.

Reflecting and Responding

1. Do a discovery Bible study on John 15:11–15.

2. What are the reasons for taking time to ask God to reveal to us His grief over our sin?

3. What are some practical ways we can "flee not flirt" with sin? How does that apply to transparency?

4. What does transparency have to do with these words of Jesus: "By this will all men know you are my disciples" (John 13:35)?

FOURTEEN

Start a Simple Church!

Church is not about maintaining committees, programs, and traditions. None of these things are wrong in themselves, but they become wrong when they keep us from the primary purpose of church, which is obeying the Great Commission (Matt. 28:19) and the Great Commandment (see Mark 12:30–31). If we are not careful, time and effort can be spent maintaining the institutions of church instead of fulfilling the main calling of the church.

If we are not careful, time and effort can be spent maintaining the institutions of church instead of fulfilling the main calling of the church.

When the life of the church centers on keeping programs running, we are no longer church as Jesus envisioned it. I'm not writing these words to encourage you to leave the church you are part of or to be critical of the church. But I am writing to alert you again to three loves of the church: worship—to love Jesus with passion and truth;

mission— to love those who don't know Jesus with courage and decency; and community—to love one another with transparency and intentionality.

Theologians would like to give us the impression that church is too complex for ordinary people to understand, but it is that very aloofness and complexity that Jesus condemned in the Pharisees. Don't make church complex or think you must have five theology degrees to obey Jesus. Jesus promised that where two or three are gathered in His name, He is there with them. He said He would build His church, so dare to let Him build it through you! Jesus came to give His church back to all His people.

Any community of Jesus followers that practices these three truths as a lifestyle is a simple church. When the three truths of worship, mission, and community are not lived out and obeyed, a local church cannot exist. Small groups that practice any one of the three can fill an important role and be effective, but that does not mean they are church. Jesus commanded us to worship Him, to take the gospel to the world, and to love one another. This is the essence of missional community.

How Do We Get It Right?

Adam, a young man I discipled while I was serving as lead pastor of a church in Kansas City, was teachable, vibrant, and spiritually hungry—but not everything I wanted to pass on clicked with him. When I used words like "evangelism" and "discipleship," something didn't connect. I often wondered if the problem was with me: What was wrong that I couldn't inspire Adam to share his faith and intentionally make disciples?

Adam confided in me recently that the problem was more about his fear of people than my inability to communicate. He said he had a misguided idea of tolerance of other people's opinions. When Adam first became a believer, he shared the good news about Jesus with others almost every day and led many people to faith in Christ. But hanging out with Christians who didn't share that same courage and commitment killed his passion. He longed to share Christ, but fear won the day.

Today, Adam is a courageous disciple-maker. He is engaging with people in his culture, yet he remains an avid follower of Jesus, connected to his culture but distinct from it at the same time. What turned him into a man of courage?

A change took place in his life so dramatic, and the fruit so wonderful, that I want to pass on what happened in Adam's own words:

Adam's Story

"I thought it would be a fairly typical Thursday evening service. That was, until I heard Angus Buchan. He is an ordinary farmer with extraordinary faith; gray-haired, energetic, and uncompromised. From the moment he started speaking I knew that he was fully in love with Jesus. This man burned with the gospel to a degree that I have never witnessed before. With tears in his eyes, Angus pleaded with the audience, 'Repent and believe in Jesus.' He spoke with conviction, authority, grace, and compassion. He understood the hour of history that we are in, the precious treasure of each heart, and he spoke as if it mattered, eternally mattered.

"His message was strong: 'Repent of your bitterness ... young man, give up your pornography ... sir, go home to your wife if you have left her.' Reminiscent of the faithful saints in history, he stood righteously before the God of heaven, grappled with men and women's eternal destiny, and declared the gospel without compromise.

"My chest got heavy; I found it hard to breathe as I dropped from my chair onto my knees, and tears streamed down my face. Questions flooded my mind. *What has been lost in my heart? What defines me? How has fear of man stolen the joy of sharing You with them? Why am I constrained by a politically correct, false gospel; a straightjacket of the fear of man that has compromised the truth and distorted Your love in me?* I had lost my passion for the kingdom and the courage that flows from loving and treasuring Jesus. It troubled me to think of dozens of believers, including myself, who hadn't led anyone to Jesus in the last five years. I was grieved, and God had my full attention.

"I had allowed the lying spirit of compromise, fear, and tolerance to whisper into my ear and win my heart for far too long. I knew God's calling on my life was to be 'a courageous heart,' and I deeply desired never to be on the wrong side again. I said yes to the Lord, to become 'Christ's ambassador,' imploring the world to be reconciled back to the Father's heart through the shed blood of the Son.

"At the end of his talk, Angus gave a call for anyone who wanted to give their whole life to Christ, and I watched as person after person of all ages came forward. I stayed bowed and asked Jesus humbly, with all the sincerity I could muster, 'Lord, will You please allow me the privilege of being part of Your harvest? Will You cause the gospel to burn in me again, and show me the ones You want to bring home to Your heart?' I sat and cried in the corner of the room where the people who'd gone forward were being talked to about their new life in Christ. I needed to be close to the joy and the wonder of men and women receiving new life in the kingdom! It stirred my longing to be part of Jesus' harvest.

"Angus was an ordinary man encountered by Jesus. He was saved in a Methodist church as I was. Angus had risked losing his entire farm by planting thousands of acres of potatoes during a drought. His faith was real, and he witnessed a miracle by bringing in a harvest of potatoes (a potato is 70 percent water) during a severe drought. As he preached the gospel, he called for people to 'plant potatoes' in the 'worst drought' they had ever had.

"My wife, Julie, and I watched this story with amazement, convicted to the core at our lack of faith and trust in God. I could feel God's tangible presence all over me as God called me to be a man of courage once again. I saw it clearly: America is in a drought—not a physical drought like Angus faced, but a spiritual drought—and I knew I was being called to sow the gospel into seemingly impossible circumstances."

Jesus' Paradoxes of Discipleship

God used a potato farmer from South Africa to reach a young man from America named Adam Cox. A paradox. Jesus works in strange ways—paradoxes—to do His work. Jesus led an upside-down disciple-making movement. He washed the disciples' feet instead of asking them to wash His. He used a young boy's lunch to feed multitudes. He gave a woman of questionable reputation the task of announcing His resurrection.

Jesus works in ways that are often counterintuitive to our way of thinking. Don't make the mistake of thinking you can improve on how Jesus made disciples. If you are serious about following Jesus, study the master. Start by gathering a few people like Jesus did, and pour your life into them. Invest in them. Be prepared for some to fall away. But keep looking for the teachable ones, and go for them!

Jesus was not after a big-meeting type of movement, led by a few super-talented leaders. He was determined to enlist a vast number of nonprofessional volunteers. He wanted a grassroots movement, not a repeat of the hierarchical institution of Judaism. He gave them freedom not to limit themselves to one day a week—the Sabbath; or to one man at the top—a priest; and one hour for worship; but to love, worship, and obey Him all week long. He modeled simplicity and gave His disciples freedom to experiment, to break away from sterile religious traditions, to learn and create, as long as they were loyal to Him and to the truth of the Scriptures that He taught them.

To help catalyze your thinking, and hopefully to help you see things through Jesus' eyes, I have summarized some of the discipleship paradoxes of Jesus below. If you can entertain and then implement the truths found in these discipleship paradoxes, you will find new ways of impacting people's lives opening up to you.

Discipleship Paradoxes

- *Jesus focused on discipling teachable nonreligious people, not those who were already religious.* Focus your energies on those not yet following Jesus. The best way to help the already saved is to model getting involved in disciple-making among the unsaved.
- *Jesus used insiders because they were more effective than outsiders.* A person inside his or her own network of friends or family is more effective in reaching those people than a highly trained,

experienced outsider. Keep religious people away from your D-Group. Go for the insiders who are in the culture, not the insiders who are already in the church.

- *Jesus discipled people to be converts; He did not convert to make disciples.* Discipleship for Jesus began when He had meaningful relationships with prebelievers. Do discipleship the way Jesus did it.

- *Jesus focused more on obedience than knowledge.* To Jesus, when you obeyed, you knew the truth. He would rather see His disciples obey one simple truth than teach them great amounts of knowledge.

- *Jesus trained a few to reach many.* Jesus knew the greatest result from His time on earth would come from reaching a few men and women and very intentionally investing in their lives.

- *Jesus went slow to go fast.* Jesus spent three years investing in a few men and women and then entrusting to them the task of reaching others.

- *Jesus entrusted the task of reaching others to those who were still new in their faith.* He didn't wait for them to be mature, fully trained, and proven.

- *Jesus expected the hardest places to yield the greatest results.* Jesus was biased toward those who didn't have choices, and He believed that when they heard, they would respond.

Generations of Spiritual Descendants

Not long ago, I received an email from a young lady in Canada who explained that she was my "spiritual granddaughter." Marissa filled me in on the story of how I not only led her father to the Lord, but that her father, in turn, had introduced her to faith in Jesus and had also led many others to faith in Christ. Her father was now pastor of a church in Ontario. She asked me if I would surprise her father (and mother) on their wedding anniversary. She wanted to introduce me to their church as well.

So I made the journey to be there for the special occasion. I showed up at the anniversary dinner party on a cold winter night in Canada. Her mother, brothers and their wives, and the associate pastor were in on the surprise. I hadn't seen Bob for many years ... it took him a few minutes to recognize me, and it took me a few minutes to gain control of my feelings. It was an emotion-filled weekend—scores of people told me that "Pastor Bob" had led them to faith in Jesus. I heard this refrain repeatedly, shared in different ways, but always the same message: "I wouldn't be here if it weren't for you. You are my spiritual grandfather."

Was it worth going through the effort of doing what I had to do to get to know Bob and share Christ with him, then spend six months investing personally in his life in a discipling relationship? Yes, it was worth everything to me, and to Bob, and to the many others who have come to faith because of his faith.

Sharing Jesus in the 1970s with Bob, a long-haired hippie dropout from Canada, while in a land filled with fanatical Taliban-type Muslim fundamentalists, is a paradox. Why did God send me from the United States to reach a Canadian in Kabul, Afghanistan? A Jesus paradox! Following Jesus is a journey that is filled with counterintuitive steps of obedience, but if we humble ourselves and allow ourselves to be led and taught by Jesus, we will discover the rich rewards of traveling with Him.

After making the long overland journey to Afghanistan to share Jesus with Bob and then—twenty-seven years later—traveling to Canada to experience the incredible blessings that my obedience had brought to Bob, his two children, and hundreds of others who are Bob's spiritual children, I am now able to relish these words Paul wrote to some of his spiritual sons and daughters:

> I responded to each of you as a caring father cares for his own children. I corrected you, encouraged you, and pleaded with you to live in such a way that our Father in heaven would be pleased with you. Do you know what gives me the greatest hope, and what I long to have as my reward when I see Jesus face to face? It is you! That's right, you are my reward! To know that you will spend eternity with Him is reward enough for me. (1 Thess. 2:9–19, author's paraphrase)

When I discipled Bob, I didn't disciple him alone. It was a community effort. Several men joined me, and we invested in his life. Although I facilitated the process and was the main one spending time with Bob, it took the combined prayers and support of a small group of people who were also determined, like me, to "make disciples." We

We wanted our lives to count for something that would last. But we also knew there were too many temptations without, and too many pressures within, to do it alone.

wanted our lives to count for something that would last. But we also knew there were too many temptations without, and too many pressures within, to do it alone.

We need other people who have the same vision and who agree on the same practices to support one another. We need the accountability and encouragement and prayer support. The early communities of believers in the book of Acts grew as networks of small disciple-making communities, meeting in homes and shops and marketplaces, rather than as large institutions maintaining programs for those already in the church. It doesn't matter to God what we call these little groups; what matters is that we meet with a few others and get serious about obeying Jesus.

Size is important if a group is to carry out mutual disciple-making. Effective large churches make disciples by mobilizing their members in outward-focused small groups. Simple churches do the same thing. Simplicity and size help keep the focus on the main mission: knowing, loving, and obeying Jesus *together*. Mutual discipleship and care cannot take place if a group grows beyond a few people. That is why being connected to a network of small discipleship groups, or to a larger congregation that has as its primary focus disciple-making in small groups, is important. We need the wisdom, resources, and accountability that a bigger community or network can provide.

How to Form and Multiply D-Groups

We call the early stages of a simple church a D-Group. A "D-Group" is a small group that has two goals: encouraging prebelievers to come to faith in Jesus, and empowering existing believers to share their faith and make disciples. D-Groups can work in existing congregations or grow into a simple church themselves. They are a great way for an existing congregation to plant more churches. They don't cost money, you don't need a building or a sound system, and they work! They are the size and type of structure that has enabled the church to explode in India and China and elsewhere in the world.

We teach that a D-Group becomes a church when they baptize their own converts and share the Lord's Supper together. (We encourage new believers to do the baptizing—they grow faster that way and take more ownership of the movement they are part of. We say, "those who evangelize—baptize.") We encourage these two things to happen within a few months of the group's inception if possible. We have learned that you don't have to pass the torch to new leaders if you never hold it in the first place! In other words, start training new leaders by modeling that leaders train leaders. In this way, the facilitator for the group is like an outside leader trying to raise up inside leaders within the group. Outside leaders are needed for many months to coach the inside leaders. We call this approach MAWL—Model, Assist, Watch, then Leave, moving on to start more D-Groups.

Successful D-Groups Have the Following Characteristics

- *Gender-based groups often work better*—it gives men and women the opportunity for transparency without fear of what members of the opposite sex think.
- *Obedience is the key*—don't try to *learn* more; try to *obey* more.
- *Short meetings of one to two hours*—once a week.

- *Follow the simple ABC format* (see below)— it makes it easy to do and easy to reproduce.
- *Leadership should be facilitative*—if there is a leader, he or she should stay in the background, while coaching others to lead the group. The ABC format keeps the group on track and makes it easy for each member of the group to start his or her own group. Take turns leading to get ready to start your own D-Group.
- *Each one starts one*—members of the group agrees at the outset that they will each share what they learn at the D-Group meeting with three to five other people between meetings, preferably prebelievers, and then as those people show interest, they start a D-Group as well.

The ABC Format of a D-Group

The secret of the ABC format is "one third, one third, one third." One third of the time is spent together praying for each other; one third of the time is spent on studying the Word, using the discovery Bible study method; and finally, one third is spent practicing what was just learned in the Bible study, with a commitment to pray for people who don't know Jesus and even to practice how they will share what they learned with someone else. Growth in a D-Group will take place by balancing emphasis on each third. Leave out one part of the format consistently, and your group will eventually stop multiplying more groups.

A—Accountability

The purpose of "A" in the first "one third" of the ABC format is to share how you did in the last week in *applying* what you learned, specifically in relationship to the passage you studied in the discovery Bible study the previous week. This includes sharing personal experiences, praying for one another, and thanking God for what He is doing in your lives. D-Groups are a great place to impart grace to one another as you share life's struggles and victories (see Deut. 6:4–9).

Here are some key questions to ask one another to facilitate the accountability time:

- How did it go this week applying what we discussed last week?
- With whom did you share last week's lesson?
- How can we pray for you to apply what God impressed on you from last week's study?

The goal for each member is grace-empowered obedience to the teachings of Jesus. To do that, you must be accountable to one another in transparent, mutual honesty. This is not a time to condemn one another but to support one another. Focus on your own obedience and victory, or on your struggle to obey and on confession of your failures, and then thank God for what He is doing in each person's life.

B—Bible study through discovery

The second "one third" of the D-Group is getting into God's Word. The way to do that, to make it interesting and engaging, is through personal, Spirit-led discovery of truth. Discovery Bible study is a way of studying the Bible where each member can participate, whether he or she is a seeker, a new believer, or someone who has been following Jesus for a long time. The goal is not to know everything about the passage; don't try to be experts by sharing or teaching lots of information—that defeats the goal of Spirit-enabled discovery. This type of Bible study allows you to discover the Word of God for yourself as the Holy Spirit teaches you.

Allow the Holy Spirit to guide you as you follow the steps below. For a list of suggested passages to study, see appendix 1, or go the personal Web site featured at the back of this book. I suggest you make a photocopy of appendix 1 and keep the list of topics and Bible passages in your Bible. Make sure everyone has an easily understood Bible translation, like the *New Living Translation.*

If you don't have a D-Group leader, ask one member to be a facilitator. The facilitator's role is to ensure that everyone has opportunity to participate and that the group stays on course with the ABC format. A facilitator can ask questions.

Read **or listen to the verses—don't teach!** See the appendixes at the back of the book for a list of suggested short passages of Scripture for various topics. For prebelievers you can start with the God Story in appendix 1. For new believers use the Seven Signs of Jesus from the gospel of John in appendix 1. Remember, focus on the passage, what it says, what it means, and what we hear God speaking to us to obey. Don't focus on opinions!

Repeat **the passage to be studied, asking one person to repeat the passage in his or her own words from memory.** One member of the D-Group can read the passage aloud. Then the facilitator can ask one member to repeat the passage in his or her own words. The key is to repeat the passage several times so that it is read, heard, and, where possible, written down, involving all the senses—seeing, hearing, speaking, and feeling. If someone misstates anything important (and it needs to be something important), the facilitator can steer the study back on course by asking, "Where did the Scripture say that…?" Your aim is for the whole group to start asking these questions as you go further in the process; allow the Word of God to teach and to correct. One way to help people do that is to ask D-Group members to insert themselves into biblical stories and imagine themselves as one of the characters, like Peter in the boat when Jesus asks him to walk on the water.

Reflect **on the passage, with the goal of each member learning one thing that applies to his or her life.** Be obedience focused! Don't worry about not understanding everything in the background or the context. The goal at this point is to hear and obey. Broader knowledge of the Scriptures can come in another setting. Take a few minutes to reflect in silence, then allow each person to share for a few minutes. (If there are long-winded people in the group, set a maximum time each person can share.) No one should share twice before each person has shared once. Focus on what each of you has learned from the verses. No "teaching" or getting on a soapbox—just personal sharing.

Report **the one thing you heard God speak—tell your D-Group members, and in the week following the study tell at least three other people what you got from the passage that applies to your life.**

C—Commitment to pray, obey, and share with others

The goal of "C" is committing yourself to obey what you learn from the Bible. Focus on what needs to be obeyed and whom you can share it with. A key ingredient to this "one third" is to review with one another what you just learned. Ask for one person to volunteer how he or she would share with a friend or neighbor what applied to his or her life from the passage. As elementary as it may sound, reporting what one is committed to obey is crucial to spiritual growth. It also builds confidence and prepares us to share with people who don't yet follow Jesus. Sounds too simple? Try it. Follow through with prayer for three to five people, known to each of you by name, with whom you desire to share Jesus. You can close, after praying, with this simple declaration: "This week, with God's help, I will …" Fill in the sentence with a commitment to obey what the Lord spoke to you from the Bible study.

Getting Started—Forming D-Groups

To get started, agree with a few people to start a D-Group, with a focus on obeying the teachings of Jesus and sharing Jesus with others who don't know Him. Make sure from the outset that you are all committed to the same thing. Read through this chapter together and discuss it. Once you have done that, set a time to meet. Form your group with two to four other believers who want to be disciples of Jesus and are committed to share with others what they are learning. Or if you want an adventure, each of you in the group can agree to look for a "person of peace" and start your own group with seeking prebelievers.

There are three very stirring results of D-Groups:

1. Seeing one another grow spiritually.

2. A new depth of friendship and community.

3. Experiencing people coming to faith in Jesus.

You can expect things to happen when you start on this pathway! Enjoy the journey, and if you need some encouragement, write to me at the email address at the back of the book or go to our Web site, where there are more resources and help to start and multiply D-Groups and simple churches. If you are looking for a way to start a simple church, follow the same steps outlined above, and seek the blessings and mentoring of a spiritual mother and father and the backing of an established local church. Remember, integrating worship, mission, and community lays the foundation for being a legitimate New Testament community. Peace and grace for the journey!

Reflecting and Responding

1. **Studying God's Word is never a superficial exercise. As you meet with your D-Group, go through the following passages to help you understand the biblical basis of the ABC format. These verses lay the foundation for what you will do in your D-Group:**

   A—Accountability—Deuteronomy 6:4–9

   B—Bible discovery—John 14:15–17

   C—Commitment to obedience—Luke 8:19–21

2. **As your D-Group grows, you can expect to discover what the church was born to be. What similarities do you find between a D-Group and the early church described in Acts 2:40–47?**

3. What lessons can you learn from my experience in discipling Bob that apply to your own life?

4. What is a discipleship paradox? What paradoxes did you see in Adam's story that might relate to your spiritual journey?

Acknowledgments

I am grateful for the assistance of dear friends and allies for their critique of this book as it was being shaped:

Guy Glass—for his watchful eye over every concept, old and new; Hamilton Stephenson—brother and coworker, for his invaluable insights and suggestions; Joan Moore—new friend and writing partner, for her editing skills; Caitlyn York—for her kindness and her eye for excellence. Thank you, Joan and Caitlyn!

I am indebted to the influence of authors who became mentors; some I have met and others I have not, some are living and some are no longer with us. I acknowledge them and their influence on my thinking and on the development of the concepts in this book. I'm grateful for the sacrifice and years that went into their books and teachings: Andrew Murray, Bob Sorge, Dietrich Bonhoeffer, C. S. Lewis, Tim Chester and Steve Timmis, Frank Viola, Leonard Sweet, L. E. Maxwell, Ron Parrish, Jimmy Seibert, Joe Ewen, David Watson, John Chen, Carl Medearis, Alan Hirsch, Michael Frost, Neil Cole, Robert Coleman, and Steve Addison.

Thank you, one and all.

APPENDIX 1

A Discovery Bible Study

To discover something is to search for it until you find it. A "discovery Bible study" works in four steps: read, restate, reflect, and report. For the discovery Bible studies in this book, use a modern translation like the NLT or *The Message*. Make three columns on a piece of paper. In one column write out the passage; rewrite it in your own words in the second column; then, as you meditate on it, list the things God speaks to you from the passage in the third column. Or, if you prefer not to write it out in three columns, do it in a discussion format with a group of friends or a Bible study group to learn the most from the passage. When you get to the "report" part of the Bible study, make sure everyone gets to share one time before anyone shares a second time. You can do a discovery Bible study with any passage of Scripture, but if you need help getting started, I suggest you work through the God Story or the Seven Signs of Jesus, below.

The God Story

Creation

There is a God and He created all that is

God creates heavens and earth	Genesis 1:1–25
God creates man and woman	Genesis 1:26–28

Truths to emphasize:

- God is the Creator but not a spirit in the creation; He is personal and infinite.
- God created humankind for three reasons: friendship with God, community with one another, and serving and caring for His creation.

Rebellion

Humankind has rebelled against God and suffered severe consequences

Rebellion in heaven	Revelation 12:7–9
Rebellion and deception on earth	Genesis 3:1–7
Guilt and shame separate God and Adam and Eve	Genesis 3:3–13
Sin and death impact everyone	Romans 3:23, 6:23

Truths to emphasize:

- Sin is rebellion and disobedience, and the penalty for our sin is spiritual death.
- God decreed death as the just punishment for sin.
- Sin grieves God and causes separation between God and man and woman.

- Satan is a liar and deceiver and will sometimes come to people in dreams or other ways.

Sacrifice

Humanity's rebellion and punishment require a substitionary sacrifice

God uses sacrifices in Old Testament as a picture of Jesus	Genesis 22:1–14
Prophecy of the death of Jesus	Isaiah 53
Jesus died in our place on the cross	Luke 24:44–47
Jesus' sacrifice was offered one time for all people	Hebrews 10:12

Truths to emphasize:

- God has provided a way to escape the penalty of sin.
- Jesus is God's sacrifice for our sins.
- There is no need for other sacrifices—Jesus is the sacrifice for all time for everyone.

Return

God provides a way for us to return to Him through repentance

God asked His people to return to Him by repenting of sin	Hosea 6:1–3
The lost son returns to his father	Luke 15:11–20
There are two things we must do to return to God	John 1:12–13
Our sins are forgiven when we return to God	1 John 1:9

Truths to emphasize:

- Returning to God is a way of acknowledging our need for forgiveness.

- Returning to God is an act of godly sorrow for our sin.
- Returning to God is asking God to forgive us and be the Lord of our lives.
- Returning to God releases God's forgiveness and restoration of friendship with God.

Commission

When we return to God we are reconciled to God and commissioned by God to tell others about His great love

When we return to God we receive new life	John 3:3–7, 15–17
God's gift of life and forgiveness is by grace	Ephesians 2:1–8
We are adopted as God's children	Romans 8:15–17
When we die we will go to heaven	Revelation 5:9–10
We become God's friends and coworkers on earth	John 15:13–16
We are sent to tell others about Jesus	Acts 1:8, Matthew 28:18–20

Truths to emphasize:
- We have assurance of salvation because of what Jesus has done for us.
- We are sent by Jesus to tell others about Him.

The Seven Signs of Jesus

Scripture List for Discovery Bible Study

Sign One: Turning water into wine—John 2:1–11

Sign Two: Healing the official's son—John 4:46–54

Sign Three: Healing the lame man—John 5:1–16

Sign Four: Feeding the five thousand—John 6:1–14

Sign Five: Calming the storm—John 6:16–27

Sign Six: Healing the man born blind—John 9:1–41

Sign Seven: Raising Lazarus from the dead—John 11:1–45

Finding a Person of Peace

A Vital Step in Starting Outreach-Focused D-Groups or Planting Simple Churches

Finding a "person of peace" is the neglected truth taught and modeled by Jesus. It is key to the growth of the church in Acts. Persons of peace hold the relational keys for unlocking doors into whole networks of people. Finding a person of peace prepared by God is a vital key to starting D-Groups and/or planting simple churches. A person of peace is sometimes recognized after the fact, but watching for such a person helps us know who we should invest valuable time in.

Jesus taught His disciples that when they went out preaching the good news, they should look for a person of peace and then focus on that person (Luke 10:5–9).

Persons of Peace Are Men or Women *Prepared by God.* They Are …

- *Welcoming* … they open their hearts and/or their homes to you.

- *Spiritually hungry* ... they are a person who has a spiritual hunger for truth and who welcomes the spreading of the good news of Jesus to their family and friends.
- *Prepared to obey Jesus* ... they are a person who goes beyond spiritual hunger to obedience.
- *Connectors* ... they are a person who provides an open door into their network of friends, their family, or their neighborhood.

Biblical Examples of the Person of Peace:

- Cornelius—Acts 10:22
- Ethiopian official—Acts 8:27
- Peter the disciple of Jesus—Luke 5:1–13
- Nicodemus—John 3:1, 7:50, 19:39
- Philippian jailer—Acts 16:25–34
- Lydia the businesswoman—Acts 16:11–15
- Mary and Martha—Luke 10:38

How Do You Find the Person of Peace?

1. Look for people to build relationships with in your sphere of influence. Watch for the person(s) God connects you to naturally who is not yet a follower of Jesus.
2. Ask around for who is the connector, networker, person of influence in a place (Matt. 10:11). That person is the one who has influence. Meet that person and if he or she is open, discuss spiritual things. See if the person is spiritually hungry.
3. Make yourself vulnerable and see who receives you (Luke 10:3–8). Speak about your interest in spiritual things.

4. See who responds to the "seed" you plant—the "good soil" person (Luke 8:4–18). Greet people, drink coffee with lots of people, and see who wants to know more.

5. Watch for those who listen and then obey the Word of God (Luke 8:21). Look for the person who takes steps to apply what he or she is learning through your one-to-one times and discovery Bible studies.

6. Look for a web of relationships in a community and find the "center," the person it revolves around.

7. Search for an influential official who welcomes the preaching of the gospel in his or her sphere of influence.

How Do You Respond to Persons of Peace?

- Focus your time investing in them—don't spread yourself too thin by focusing on too many people (Luke 10:7).

- Spend time with them in the context of their friends and relationships (5:1–13).

- Listen to their story and tell them your faith story of coming to Jesus.

- Accept them as they are (19:1–8).

- Let them help you as well—be open to learn from them (10:7–8).

- Share the good news of Jesus and minister to their practical needs (10:9).

- Meet in their home or where they gather with friends (10:5).

- A person of peace doesn't always come to faith in Jesus but they do open doors to others (John 3).

Becoming a D-Group Starter

D-groups are discipleship groups that can grow into simple churches or remain small groups in a local church. The key element of D-Groups is multiplication—that is what gets people active in being a disciple and making disciples. Realistically, some D-Groups will fail. Don't try to rescue them if that is the case.

Focus your energy on coaching those that are willing to train others to lead the groups and are active in multiplying more groups. Focus where the life is, where there are people who want to share their faith and who long to grow spiritually.

Three Key Elements to Multiplying D-Groups:

1. Stick to the ABC pattern. The process is very important, and your job as a coach is to make sure the process stays on course. Don't be fanatical about the model, but learn the principles that make the model work, and then be flexible.

2. Hand over quickly to a new facilitator. Use the MAWL process the following way:

Model—Model the ABC process three times (not more), then turn it over. As you model, ask your potential facilitator, "Did you see what I did? Do you think you could do it?" This allows your facilitator-in-training to realize you are modeling something you want him or her to catch!

Assist—From the fourth time the group comes together, the new facilitator takes over. At this point you assist by keeping the process on track. You also meet with your facilitator to brief and debrief him or her on how he or she is doing.

Watch—You no longer have to keep the process on track, because your facilitator has got it! You miss some of the meetings to start more D-Groups.

Leave—The group no longer depends on you to run. You continue to mentor your facilitator at a separate time.

3. Try not to allow people to join the group once it's going. Focus on starting new groups wherever possible. When new people want to join, start new groups with them!

How to Start and Coach a New D-Group:

- Pray for the right people—wait until you find them!
- Start by doing the ABCs together.
- Pray a lot more!
- Look for natural ways to gain access to the community and people you want to impact—do the things you enjoy in life, but do them with intentionality to share Jesus.
- Look for the "person of peace" (Luke 10:1–11).
- Get involved in the person of peace's network or family—but

don't get overly impressed with the first friendly person you meet.

- Start the discovery study in someone's home in the community (it may be with as few as two to four people).
- Choose someone to be the facilitator from the very first time you meet, then coach that person following the MAWL process.
- Work toward multiplication by starting new D-Groups as people want to join the group.

D-Group "No-No's"

- Don't take offerings for ministries or projects.
- Don't recruit volunteers for other projects or ministries.
- Don't get distracted by discussions about someone's personal doctrine.
- Don't mix personal business with discipleship.
- Don't mix politics with your D-Group.
- Don't be a matchmaker of relationships.
- Don't turn it into a personal accountability group.
- Don't spend time alone counseling or driving members of the opposite sex.
- Don't borrow or lend money to persons in the group.
- Don't invite guest speakers.

Notes

Introduction: Simple Yet Profound
1. Waylon Moore, *Multiplying Disciples* (Colorado Springs, CO: NavPress, 1981), 21.
2. Michael Frost and Alan Hirsch, *ReJesus* (Peabody, MA: Hendrickson, 2009), 6.
3. Ibid., 8.
4. Ibid., 8.

Chapter 2: Obedience
1. Dietrich Bonhoeffer, *The Cost of Discipleship* (New York: Macmillan, 1959), 339.
2. Ibid.
3. Frost and Hirsch, *ReJesus*, 13.
4. These insights are adapted from Dietrich Bonhoeffer, *The Cost of Discipleship*, 344.

Chapter 3: Lordship
1. Frost and Hirsch, *ReJesus*, 20.

Chapter 4: Repentence
1. L. E. Maxwell, *Born Crucified* (Chicago: Moody Press, 1984).

Chapter 5: Pride
1. C. S. Lewis, *Mere Christianity* (New York: Macmillian, 1964).

Chapter 6: Faithfulness
1. Steve Addison tells the story of Patrick in his book *Movements That Change the*

World (Smyrna, DE: Missional Press, 2009). I have adapted the story of Patrick from Steve's book, in some places quoting from Steve and in others taking the liberty of giving my own perspective.

Chapter 7: Prayer

1. Bob Sorge, *Secrets of the Secret Place* (Hatfield, South Africa: Van Schaik Publishers, 2000); Pete Greig, *God on Mute* (Ventura, CA: Regal, 2007).

2. See Chuck Quinley, *The Quest* (Kennesaw, GA: Emerge Missions, Inc., 2008), 44. For more information go to www.thequestonline.net.

Chapter 8: Practicing Jesus

1. Frank Viola and Leonard Sweet, "A Magna Carta for Restoring the Supremacy of Jesus Christ," A Jesus Manifesto, http://ajesusmanifesto.wordpress.com (accessed June 22, 2009).

2. In the paragraphs that follow I am adapting the helpful insights of Leonard Sweet and Frank Viola in *The Jesus Manifesto* (Nashville: Thomas Nelson, 2010).

3. Viola and Sweet, "A Magna Carta for Restoring the Supremacy of Jesus Christ."

Chapter 9: Sharing Jesus

1. Tim Chester and Steve Timmis, *Total Church* (Wheaton, IL: Crossway, 2008), 65.

Chapter 10: Suffering with Jesus

1. Bonhoeffer, *The Cost of Discipleship*, 99.

Chapter 11: Committed Community

1. Chester and Timmis, *Total Church*, 39.

Chapter 12: Allies in a Global Awakening

1. Steve Addison, *Movements That Change the World*, 70.

2. Ibid., 119.

To learn more about All Nations
and
Floyd and Sally's work in Africa
please visit their Web site at
www.floydandsally.org
or go to
www.all-nations.co.za

Opportunities to join them include ...
Short-Term Teams
Internships
CPx—Leadership and Church-Planting Training

For more information, write to
info@all-nations.co.za

To follow Floyd on Twitter search for Floyd
McClung or find him @floydandsally